Supplements Sampler
for

Hoy día

McMinn • Alonso García

Prentice Hall
is an imprint of

Upper Saddle River, New Jersey 07458

Prentice Hall
is an imprint of

© 2011 by PEARSON EDUCATION, INC.
Upper Saddle River, New Jersey 07458

ISBN-13: 978-0-205-78494-3
ISBN-10: 0-205-78494-1

Printed in the United States of America

Introduction

Dear Instructor:

Welcome to *Hoy día!*

Hoy día: **Spanish for Real Life** is the text for today's instructors, students, and classroom. *Hoy día* focuses on Spanish students' need for everyday communication. It teaches them to function in a variety of real-world settings--at work and in their neighborhoods, traveling abroad or doing service in their local communities. *Hoy día* helps students focus on what they need to know to use Spanish effectively in real life. As Spanish becomes more and more indispensable in daily life, students will find *Hoy día*: **Spanish for Real Life** an excellent tool that facilitates both their immersion in the Spanish language and their connection to the people who speak it.

Within this sampler you will find a sample of our key supplements that correspond with Chapter 2 of the textbook. Please note that not all supplements are included in this sampler (e.g., the Answer Key for the Student Activities Manual). If you would like to receive a complete copy of any of the supplements, your Pearson Sales Representative will be happy to supply you with this.

At the front of this booklet you will also find a CD-Rom that contains samples of the majority of the *Hoy día* media components.

Enjoy!

Pearson-Prentice Hall World Languages

Contents

Instructor's Resource Manual

∾

John T. McMinn - *Austin Community College*
Nuria Alonso García - *Providence College*

The **Hoy día** IRM is a comprehensive resource that instructors can use for a variety of purposes. In the following page you will find a complete list of its contents. Here are some highlights:

■ An introduction that discusses the features of the new edition and includes a guide to the supplements.

■ An explanation of the North American educational system, written (in Spanish) for instructors who may be unfamiliar with it.

■ Pointers for new instructors, including tips on lesson planning and classroom management.

■ Sample syllabi and detailed lesson plans showing how the **Hoy día** program can be used in different educational settings and at different paces.

■ Rubrics for written and oral assessment.

Hoy día
Instructor's Resource Manual

Table of Contents

Hoy día

Traditional (face-to-face) Syllabus
Two-semester program: 6 chapters per semester (12 chapters total)
Four 50-minute class meetings per week (9-10 days per chapter followed by chapter exam)

<u>Semester I</u>

Demo: Chapter 2

Day	Chapter	Class objective	In-class assignments	Homework Student Activities Manual
1	**2 - *Después de clase*** **Tema 1: Vocabulario**	Talk about the concept of time, schedules and leisure activities	*Mi horario* Assignments: *Una conversación* and 2-1 to 2-3, p. 37	2-1 to 2-4, pp. 27-29
	Tema 1: Gramática 1	Introduce time expressions and calendar	*Describing your schedule: Time and days of the week* Assignments: 2-4 to 2-7, p. 39	2-5 to 2-9, pp. 30-32
2	**Tema 1: Gramática 2**	Locate people and places using the verb ***estar*** and adverbs of frequency	*Saying where you are: The verb **estar*** Assignments: 2-8 to 2-10, pp. 40-41	2-10 to 2-14, pp. 33-34
	Tema 2: Vocabulario	Exchange information about leisure time and activities in the Hispanic world	*Las actividades diarias* Assignments: *Una conversación* and 2-11 to 2-13, p. 43	2-15 to 2-18, pp. 35-36

3	**Tema 2: Gramática 1**	Practice regular *-ar* verbs in the present tense	*Talking about your activities: Regular –ar verbs* Assignments: 2-14 to 2-16, p. 45	2-19 to 2-21, pp. 37-38
	Tema 2: Gramática 2	Ask and answer questions	*Asking questions: Question formation* Assignments: 2-17 to 2-19, p. 47	2-22 to 2-27, pp. 38-40
4	**Tema 3: Vocabulario**	Indicate locations close to the university	*Lugares cerca de la universidad* Assignments: *Una conversación* and 2-20 to 2-23, p. 49	2-28 to 2-30, pp. 40-42
	Tema 3: Gramática 1		*Indicating location: prepositions of place and contractions with de* Assignments: 2-24 to 2-27, pp. 50-51	2-31 to 2-33, pp. 42-44
5	**Tema 3: Gramática 2**	Talk about things that will happen in the near future, using the construction of *ir a +* infinitive	*Saying what you are going to do; ir, contractions with a, ir a + infinitive* Assignments: 2-28 to 2-32, p. 52-53	2-34 to 2-36, p. 45
	Tema 4: Vocabulario	Hobbies and leisure activities	*Los pasatiempos* Assignments: *Una conversación* and 2-33 to 2-36, p. 55	2-37 to 2-40, pp. 46-47
6	**Tema 4: Resumen de gramática**	Real-life simulation of working in the Hispanic Chamber of Commerce	*En la vida real* Assignments: 2-37 to 2-42 and *Entre profesionales*, pp. 58-59	
	Hoy día	Cultural contact:		

		Reading (Guessing meaning from context)	**Lectores de hoy**: *Moda global* Assignments: 2-43 to 2-47, pp. 60-61	2-53 to 2-55, pp. 54-55
7	**Hoy día**	Cultural contact: Listening (Identifying the main idea) and Writing (Brainstorming)	**Voces de la calle:** *Centros sociales comunitiarios* Assignments: 2-48 to 2-51, p. 62 **Escritores en acción:** *Tu perfil en Internet* Assignments: 2-52 to 2-56, p. 63	2-56 to 2-57, pp. 55-56 2-58, p. 56
8		Review *Capítulo 2*	*Resumen de gramática*, pp. 56-57 *Vocabulario,* pp. 64-65 Additional resources in MySpanishLab: Mnemonic dictionary and *Escapadas*	2-41 to 2-51, pp. 48-53
9			***Capítulo 2* Test**	

Hoy día
Hybrid (online and face-to-face) Syllabus

Two-semester program: 6 chapters per semester (12 chapters total)
Two 50-minute class meetings per week and two online sessions per week (9-10 days per chapter followed by chapter test)

Semester I

Demo: Chapter 2

Day	Chapter	Class objective	In-class assignments	Homework Student Activities Manual	MySpanishLab Tutorials
1	**2 - *Después de clase* Tema 1: Vocabulario** **Tema 1: Gramática 1**	Talk about the concept of time, schedules and leisure activities Introduce time expressions and calendar	*Mi horario* Assignments: *Una conversación* and 2-1 to 2-3, p. 37 *Describing your schedule: Time and days of the week* Assignments: 2-4 to 2-7, p. 39	2-1 to 2-4, pp. 27-29 2-5 to 2-9, pp. 30-32	
2 Online	**Tema 1: Gramática 2** **Tema 2: Vocabulario**	Locate people and places using the verb ***estar*** and adverbs of frequency Exchange information about leisure time and activities in the Hispanic world	*Saying where you are: The verb **estar*** Assignments: 2-8 to 2-10, pp. 40-41 *Las actividades diarias* Assignments: *Una conversación* and 2-11 to 2-13, p. 43	2-10 to 2-14, pp. 33-34 2-15 to 2-18, pp. 35-36	Spanish Grammar Tutorial: Subject pronouns Spanish Grammar Tutorial: Estar
3	**Tema 2: Gramática 1**	Practice regular -*ar* verbs in the present tense	*Talking about your activities: Regular –**ar** verbs* Assignments: 2-14	2-19 to 2-21,	Spanish Grammar Tutorial: Subject pronouns Spanish Grammar

Day	Chapter	Class objective	In-class assignments	Homework Student Activities Manual	MySpanishLab Tutorials
	Tema 2: Gramática 2	Ask and answer questions	to 2-16, p. 45 *Asking questions: Question formation* Assignments: 2-17 to 2-19, p. 47	pp. 37-38 2-22 to 2-27, pp. 38-40	Tutorial: -ar verbs Spanish Grammar Tutorial: Formation of Negative Sentences Spanish Grammar Tutorial: Questions with interrogative words
4 Online	Tema 3: Vocabulario Tema 3: Gramática 1	Indicate locations close to the university	*Lugares cerca de la universidad* Assignments: *Una conversación* and 2-20 to 2-23, p. 49 *Indicating location: prepositions of place and contractions with de* Assignments: 2-24 to 2-27, pp. 50-51	2-28 to 2-30, pp. 40-42 2-31 to 2-33, pp. 42-44	
5	Tema 3: Gramática 2 Tema 4: Vocabulario	Talk about things that will happen in the near future, using the construction of *ir a* + infinitive Hobbies and leisure activities	*Saying what you are going to do; ir, contractions with a, ir a + infinitive* Assignments: 2-28 to 2-32, p. 52-53 *Los pasatiempos* Assignments: *Una conversación* and 2-33 to 2-36, p. 55	2-34 to 2-36, p. 45 2-37 to 2-40, pp. 46-47	Spanish Grammar Tutorial: Future with ir + a + infinitive Spanish Grammar Tutorial: Preposition a

Day	Chapter	Class objective	In-class assignments	Homework Student Activities Manual	MySpanishLab Tutorials
6 Online	**Tema 4: Resumen de gramática**	Real-life simulation of working in the Hispanic Chamber of Commerce	*En la vida real* Assignments: 2-37 to 2-42 and *Entre profesionales*, pp. 58-59		
	Hoy día	Cultural contact: Reading (Guessing meaning from context)	**Lectores de hoy:** *Moda global* Assignments: 2-43 to 2-47, pp. 60-61	2-53 to 2-55, pp. 54-55	
7	**Hoy día**	Cultural contact: Listening (Identifying the main idea) and Writing (Brainstorming)	**Voces de la calle:** *Centros sociales comunitiarios* Assignments: 2-48 to 2-51, p. 62	2-56 to 2-57, pp. 55-56	
			Escritores en acción: *Tu perfil en Internet* Assignments: 2-52 to 2-56, p. 63	2-58, p. 56	
8 Online		Review *Capítulo 2*	*Resumen de gramática*, pp. 56-57	2-41 to 2-51, pp. 48-53	
			Vocabulario, pp. 64-65		
			Additional resources in MySpanishLab: Mnemonic dictionary and *Escapadas*		

Day	Chapter	Class objective	In-class assignments	Homework Student Activities Manual	MySpanishLab Tutorials
9			*Capítulo 2* Test		

Hoy día
Traditional Lesson Plans

Two-semester program: 6 chapters per semester (12 chapters total)
Four 50-minute class meetings per week (9-10 days per chapter followed by chapter exam)

SEMESTER I

Demo: Capítulo 2: *Después de clase*

Day 1
Objectives: Introduce the concept of time, schedules and leisure activities and places
Topics: Tema 1 Vocabulario, Gramática 1
Materials: Textbook, pictures/ props, video

Activity	Time allotted for activity	Class Activity	Textbook activities
1	15 Minutes	- Greet students and ask them how they are doing in Spanish. -Introduction to the chapter. Present the chapter theme and review the cultural information presented in the chapter opener. - Introduction to the Vocabulary. Write on the board the following questions: 1. *¿Qué día es hoy?* 2. *¿Qué hora es?* 3. *¿A qué hora es la clase de español?* 4. *¿Qué clases tomas los lunes, miércoles y viernes a las diez de la mañana?* 5. *¿Qué haces* (what do you do) *los viernes por la noche?* - Objectives: Introduce the 2 main points of today's class and its objectives, as stated on the syllabus then, proceed to answer the first question *Hoy es lunes 5 de octubre, 2009.* Mention that the Spanish calendar starts with Monday and ends with Sunday, and that the days of the week and the months of the year are not capitalized in Spanish, as they are in English. - Oral & Written Practice: Activity *Una conversación* and 2-3 *Otra conversacíon.* Because of time constraints, the instructor may want to mention in the	*Una conversación,* **2-1 to 2-3**

1		previous class that *Una conversación* should be studied before coming to class, therefore, the new vocabulary and grammatical structures are clear.	
2	10 Minutes	- Explain the use of the definite article *el* or *los* in front of the days of the week *(el/ los lunes)* to refer to repetitive actions on certain days. Oral & Written Practice: Use different clocks/ watches at different times (these could be toys or pictures). Ask students to tell the time, by using *y (cuarto) and menos (cuarto)* for the minutes. - Explain that time is femenine in Spanish and the reason why we use *la una y las dos…* - Clarify the difference between "what time is it?" and "at what time does an activity take place?"	**2-4 to 2-5**
3	10 Minutes	Communicative Exercise: You may consider using the Supplemental activity on p. 38, so students can practice the days of the week: Distribute copies of daily planners for a week and ask students to take turns describing their class and work schedules using different times and days of the week. In addition to producing complete sentences, pay attention to students' pronunciation of *mi<u>é</u>rcoles* and *s<u>á</u>bado* where the accent is usually misplaced.	
4	5 Minutes	Assessment on written exercises: Correct the assigned written activities on the syllabus, and collect the assignments.	
5	5 Minutes	- **Option 1.** Listening Comprehension: Assign *¡A escuchar!* (CD 1 Track 27), with books closed then, with books opened to assess students' listening and comprehension skills. - **Option 2** Communicative Exercise: Correct Activity 2-6 *Entrevista* This pair activity will be practiced in class orally. The instructor may collect the written version of this activity assignment to assess the proper use of *gustar* verb. *If time does not allow, the instructor may well	***¡A escuchar!*** **2-6**

5		consider starting the next class with the *Entrevista* activity.	
6	5 Minutes	- <u>Final Summary</u>: Review the *¡Ojo!* box and do 2-7 *Comparaciones culturales* to practice converting from a 24-hour clock to a 12-hour clock. Review the new concepts of time, days of the week, and leisure activities and places that are written on the board. Ask students if they are clear and if they have any questions. - Ask students to review the self-check questions in *Para averiguar* or you may wish to use them to quickly check that students have understood the explanations. Repeat selected expressions and correct their pronunciation. - Take-leave in Spanish, and remind them to follow the instructions on the syllabus, and have their assignments completed before coming to class.	**2-7**

<u>Homework</u>:

1. Instructors may remind their students that they should plan on studying at least two hours for every hour in class. Students may be advised that they are expected to do all the activities before coming to class, as stated earlier on the syllabus.

2. Instructors may also advise their students to follow up with the contents and requirements of the syllabus, as stated for each day of the week.

3. Do SAM 2-1 to 2-9

Day 2

<u>Objectives</u>: Introduce the verb *estar* and locations, subject pronouns, and adverbs of frequency
<u>Topics</u>: Tema 1. Gramática 2
<u>Materials</u>: Textbook, pictures/ props, video

Activity	Time allotted for activity	Class Activity	Textbook activities
1	15 Minutes	- Greet students and ask them how they are doing in Spanish. - Introduce the verb *estar.* Write on the board the following questions: 1. *¿Cómo estás? 2. ¿Dónde estás ahora? 3. ¿Estás en clase todos los días?* - <u>Objectives</u>: Introduce the main points of today's class and its objectives, as stated on the syllabus. Answer the first question *Estoy muy bien, gracias.* Mention that this is the second verb *to be* in Spanish and it has several uses. These are just two of them: emotional/ physical states, and location. For location, explain that the verb *estar* is usually used with the preposition *en (Ahora estamos en la clase de español).* - <u>Oral & Written Practice</u>: Proceed to the adverbs of frequency. Make the students listen and repeat, so that they are able to practice new words and sounds.	**2-8 to 2-10**
2	10 minutes	-<u>Introduce Vocabulary</u>: *Las actividades diarias* - Explain the conjugation of the verb *gustar* and its use with daily / or leisure activities. *¿Qué te gusta hacer los sábados por la noche?* - Clarify that the verb *gustar* could be either followed by a singular or plural noun, or by one or several verbs in infinitive. *Me gusta la coca-cola"; "A mi novio, le gustan las papas fritas"; "A mi padre le gusta mirar el fútbol.* - <u>Listening Comprehension Practice</u>: You may assign *Una conversación* (CD 1, Track 29). As suggested, have students listen and comprehend the	***Una conversación, ¡A escuchar!***

2		conversation first with their books closed, then allow them to open their books and look for the correct answers. Then, *¡A escuchar!,*(CD 1, Track 30) - <u>Oral & Written Practice</u>: By looking at the pictures on page 42, have students ask and respond to each other about their plans after class and in the weekends.	**2-11 to 2-12**
3	10 Minutes	- <u>Communicative Exercise</u>: Assign pairs to practice 2-13 *Otra conversación.* Students will have the opportunity to exchange ideas, and incorporate the new vocabulary and grammatical structures	**2-13**
4	5 Minutes	- <u>Instructor's Assessment on Written Exercises</u>: Correct individually the assigned oral/ written activities on the syllabus, and collect the assignments. ** It should be stated clearly on the syllabus that the instructor "may/ may not collect the assigned homework", and "may/ may not announce a quiz".	
5	5 Minutes	- <u>Final Summary</u>: Go over the verb **estar**, locations and adverbs of frequency. Also, go over the use of the verb **gustar.** Ask students if they are clear and if they have any questions. - Ask students to repeat selected expressions and correct their pronunciation. Finally, ask them to provide the correct answers again. - Take-leave in Spanish, and remind them to follow the instructions on the syllabus, and have their assignments completed before coming to class.	
6	5 Minutes	- <u>Final Summary</u>: Review the new concepts of time, days of the week, and leisure activities and places that are written on the board. Ask students if they are clear and if they have any questions. - Ask students to repeat selected expressions and correct their pronunciation. Finally, ask them to provide the correct answers again. - Take-leave in Spanish, and remind them to follow the instructions on the syllabus, and have their assignments completed before coming to class.	

<u>Homework</u>:
1. Do SAM 2-10 to 2-18

Day 3

<u>Objectives</u>: Introduce the **–ar** verbs in the present tense; ask and answer questions, and talk about your activities

<u>Topics</u>: Tema 2 Gramática 2

<u>Materials</u>: Textbook, pictures/ props, video

Activity	Time allotted for activity	Class Activity	Textbook activities
1	15 Minutes	- Write on the board the following questions: 1. *¿Cocinas todos los días? 2. ¿Con qué frecuencia miras la televisión? 3. ¿Estudias más en casa o en la biblioteca?* - Greet students and ask them if they have any questions. You may also want to allow students time to practice 2-12 *¿Y tú?* or 2-13 *Otra conversación* with a partner. - <u>Objectives</u>: Introduce the main points of today's class and its objectives, as stated on the syllabus then, proceed to answer the questions 1. *"Sí, cocino todos los días"*, 2. *"Miro la televisión todas las tardes"*, 3. *No, estudio más en la biblioteca"*. - <u>Introduction to *Gramática 1*</u>. The (-ar) verbs in the present tense. Clarify that the Spanish verbs are classified in 3 categories (-ar), (-er), and (-ir) verbs. - Go over the verb conjugation with all the subject pronouns and introduce the other verbs from the list in context (p. 44). Also clarify the difference between the affirmative and the negative forms. - <u>Oral & Written Practice</u>: You may assign 2-14 to 2-16 (if time allows).	**2-14 to 2-16**
2	15 Minutes	- Introduce Question Formation in Spanish. Explain the different ways Spanish-speaking people ask questions: 1. By raising their intonation in a statement, 2. By switching the order of the verb-subject, 3. By using a tag question, 4. By using interrogative words	

2		- <u>Oral & Written Practice</u>: You may consider using the Supplemental Activity on p. 46.	**2-17 to 2-19**
3	10 minutes	- <u>Instructor's Assessment on Communicative and Written Exercises</u>: Correct individually the assigned oral/ written activities and collect the assignments ** It should be stated previously on the syllabus that the instructor may/ may not collect the assigned homework, and may/ may not announce a quiz.	
4	10 minutes	- <u>Final Summary</u>: Go over the (-ar) verbs in the present tense, and the Question Formation. Ask students if they are clear and if they have any questions. - Ask students to review the self-check questions in *Para averiguar* or you may wish to use them to quickly check that students have understood the explanations. - Take-leave in Spanish, and remind them to follow the instructions on the syllabus, and have their assignments completed before coming to class.	

<u>Homework:</u>
1. Do SAM 2-19 to 2-27

Day 4

<u>Objectives</u>: Indicating locations close to the university, and use of prepositions of place and contractions with *de*

<u>Topics</u>: Tema 3. Vocabulario, Gramática 2

<u>Materials</u>: Textbook, pictures/ props, video

Activity	Time allotted for activity	Class Activity	Textbook activities
1	15 Minutes	- Greet students and ask them how they are doing in Spanish. - <u>Introduction to Vocabulario</u>: *Lugares cerca de la Universidad* - Use "Supplemental Activity" as a warm-up exercise. - You may also ask students *"¿Qué hay en tu ciudad?, ¿Qué lugares hay para divertirse?* (have fun), based on the illustrations provided on page 48. - Indirectly, you may explain the verb auxiliary *haber* - Write on the board the answers of the students, and make sure that their spelling and pronunciation are correct. - <u>Objectives</u>: Introduce the new vocabulary in context and its objectives, as stated on the syllabus - <u>Listening Comprehension Practice</u>: You may assign *Una conversación* and *¡A escuchar!* (CD 1 Tracks 32 and 33). Follow the steps that are suggested, by asking students to listen and answer the questions with their books closed first, then with their books open, in order to double-check their comprehension and to ultimately correct themselves.	**2-21 to 2-22** *Una conversación* *¡A escuchar!*
2	15 minutes	-<u>Introduce Gramática 1</u> - Go over the list of prepositions and the use of *de*, *del* (+ masculine singular noun), and *de la* (+feminine singular noun, 50) - <u>Oral & Written Practice</u>: You may consider using the Supplemental Activity on page 50. - You may also use activity 2-26 *En la calle Molino*	**2-24 to 2-27**

3	15 Minutes	- <u>Instructor's Assessment on Communicative and Written Exercises</u>: Correct individually the assigned oral/ written activities on the syllabus, and collect the assignments.	
4	5 Minutes	- <u>Final Summary</u>: Go over the new vocabulary and the prepositions of place and contractions with *de*. Ask students if they are clear and if they have any questions. - Ask students to repeat selected expressions and correct their pronunciation. Finally, ask them to provide the correct answers again. - Take-leave in Spanish, and remind them to follow the instructions on the syllabus, and have their assignments completed before coming to class.	

<u>Homework</u>:
1. Do SAM 2-28 to 2-33

Day 5

<u>Objectives</u>: Saying what you are going to do, using the verb *"ir"* and *"ir"* a + infinitive, contractions with *a*, and Los pasatiempos;

<u>Topics</u>: Tema 3 Gramática 2, Tema 4 Vocabulario

<u>Materials</u>: Textbook, pictures/ props, video

Activity	Time allotted for activity	Class Activity	Textbook activities
1	15 minutes	- <u>Objectives</u>: Introduce the verb *ir* in context of location and its use to indicate "near future", as stated on the syllabus. - Greet students and ask them if they have any questions. Do a quick comprehension check using 2-25 to assess whether students have understood the material. You may also want to allow students time to practice 2-26 with a partner. - <u>Conjugation of the verb *Ir* in the present tense</u>. Indicate its irregular nature as a verb. - Talk about things that are going to happen in the near future, by using *ir a* + infinitive and adverbs of time *esta tarde", "la semana que viene"*. - Ask students about their plans next weekend: where they are going, and what they are going to do. Write on the board their answers, and make sure that their pronunciation and grammatical structures are correct.	**2-28 to 2-32**
2	15 minutes	- <u>Introduce Vocabulario: Los pasatiempos</u> (54) Review the *(-ar)* verbs, the verb *ir* and locations, while introducing hobbies and leisure activities - <u>Listening Comprehension Practice</u>: You may consider using *¡A escuchar!* (CD 1 Track 36), p. 55. As suggested, have students listen and comprehend the conversation first with their books closed, then allow them to open their books and look for the correct answers.	**2-34 to 2-35** Tema 4. *¡A escuchar!*, **p. 55**
3	15 minutes	- <u>Introduce Vocabulary</u>: *Los pasatiempos*	**2-33 to 2-34**

3		Review the (-ar) verbs, the verb *ir* and locations, while introducing hobbies and leisure activities. - <u>Listening Comprehension Practice</u>: You may assign *Una conversación* (CD 1, Track 35). As suggested, have students listen and comprehend the conversation first with their books closed, then allow them to open their books and look for the correct answers. Then, *¡A escuchar!,*(CD 1, Track 36)	***Una conversación, ¡A escuchar!***
4	10 minutes	- <u>Communicative Exercise</u> -Assign 2-35 *Otra conversación* and have students practice with a partner. You may have pairs present their conversations for the class.	**2-35**
5	10 minutes	- <u>Final Summary</u>: Go over the verb *ir,* the new vocabulary, and the reading(s). Ask students if they are clear and if they have any questions. -Ask students to review the self-check questions in *Para averiguar* or you may wish to use them to quickly check that students have understood the explanations. - Take-leave in Spanish, and remind them to follow the instructions on the syllabus, and have their assignments completed before coming to class.	

<u>Homework</u>:
1. Do SAM 2-34 to 2-40

Day 6
Objectives: Culural contacts with social realities
Topics: Voces de la calle,
Materials: Textbook, pictures/ props, video

Activity	Time allotted for activity	Class Activity	Textbook activities
1	20 Minutes	- Greet students and ask them how they are doing in Spanish. -Review *Resumen de gramática* -You can either assign the *Resumen de gramática* to be reviewed at home or you can quickly review the main points using questions form *Para averiguar* boxes. - Introduce *En la vida real* -Present the real-life scenario for *En la vida real* (workir in the Hispanic Chamber of Commerce). - Have students practice activity 2-39 *¿Y tú?* and 2-42 with a partner. You may ask pairs to present the activit to the class or have them report back what they learne from their partner. -Encourage students to visit MySpanishLab for more *Entre profesionales* vocabulary and activities related to professions and careers.	**2-37 to 2-42**
2	15 minutes	-Introduce reading selection for *Lectores de hoy* -Review the reading strategy in *Antes de leer*. Read *Moda global* and have students complete the activities in *Ahora tú* and *Después de leer*.	**2-53 to 2-55**
3	5 Minutes	- Final Summary: Go over the verb *ir*, the new vocabulary, and the main messages of the reading(s). Ask students if they are clear and if they have any questions. - Assess students' assigned written activities. - Take-leave in Spanish, and remind them to follow the instructions on the syllabus, and have their assignments completed before coming to class.	

1. Do SAM 2-53 to 2-55

Day 7

<u>Objectives</u>: Cultural contact: listening , viewing, speaking and writing

<u>Topics</u>: Voces de la calle and Escritores en acción

<u>Materials</u>: Textbook, pictures/ props, video

Activity	Time allotted for activity	Class Activity	Textbook activities
1	10 minutes	- Greet students and ask them how they are doing in Spanish. Do a quick warm-up with 2-42 *Mi restaurante favorite*. You may also want to allow students time to practice 2-26 with a partner. - <u>Objectives</u>: Cultural contact: listening , viewing, speaking and writing about social, artistic and political projects where students can participate in, and make a difference in their own community and society	
2	15 minutes	- **Option 1**. -<u>Introduce </u>*Voces de la calle: Centros sociales comunitarios* - Make a link between the verb *ir* and its use in the near future and the cultural component about civic engagement, and ask students to predict one social commitment -You can have students view the video in class or assign for homework. - **Option 2**. -<u>Introduce </u>*Escritores en acción: Tu perfil en internet* You may use the writing strategies, as suggested, in order to invite students to think and to write about their personal profile in myspace.latino. This is an engaging activity that aims at reviewing the new vocabulary of schedules, hobbies and leisure, the (-*ar*) verbs, the verb *gustar,* the verb *ir,* the verb *estar* and locations, and other relevant information of self description and qualities. - At the end, students may exchange their creative work with other students and with their instructor, for constructive feedback and evaluation of content, style and creativity	2-48 to 2-51 2-52 to 2-56
3	15 minutes	<u>Sample Exam.</u> As an effective practice, instructors may consider giving their students an exam (from the	

Activity	Time allotted for activity	Class Activity	Textbook activities
3		exam bank) which contemplates reading, writing, and listening skills. This is a good practice before the chapter exam	
4	5 minutes	- <u>Final Summary</u>: Review the main components of chapter 2. Ask students if they are clear and if they have any questions. - Take-leave in Spanish, and remind them to study for the exam the next class day.	

<u>Homework:</u>
1. Do SAM 2- 56 to 2-58

Day 8

<u>Objectives</u>: General review of the vocabulary, grammar and culture of *Capítulo 2*
<u>Topics</u>: Tema 1-Tema 4; Resumen de Gramática, Vocabulario
<u>Materials</u>: Textbook, pictures/ props, video

Activity	Time allotted for activity	Class Activity	Textbook activities
1	10 minutes	Prepare students for *Capítulo* 2 Exam: *Después de clase.* Begin the review by asking students if they have any questions or need additional clarification from any of the chapter structures and vocabulary or any of the homework activities.	
2	25 minutes	-Review grammar in *Resumen de gramática* and be certain that all verb conjugations and sentence structures are clear. -Review vocabulary using the end vocabulary list and ask students to use the new words and expressions properly in complete and coherent sentences or paragraphs. Encourage students to visit the Mnemonic Dictionary online as an additional study aid. You may also use this time to address to complete any textbook activities you may not have had time to practice.	
3	15 minutes	<u>Sample Exam.</u> As an effective practice, instructors may consider giving their students an exam (from the exam bank) which contemplates reading, writing, and listening skills. This is a good practice before the chapter exam	

<u>Homework</u>:
1. Do SAM 2- 41 to 2-51

Day 9
Objectives: Assessment of chapter vocabulary, grammar and culture
Topics: *Capítulo 2* Test
Materials: Test

Activity	Time allotted for activity	Class Activity	Textbook activities
1	5 minutes	- Greet students and do a quick review using questions from the *Para averiguar* boxes.	
2	40 minutes	*Capítulo 2* Test	
3	5 minutes	-Introduction to *Capítulo 3.* Use the last few minutes of class to present the chapter theme and review the cultural information presented in the chapter opener.	

Homework:
1. Review cultural information presented in chapter opener of *Capítulo 3*, p. 67
2. Do SAM 3-1 to 3-4

Hoy día
Hybrid (online and face-to-face) Lesson Plans

Two-semester program: 6 chapters per semester (12 chapters total)
Two 50-minute class meetings per week and two online sessions per week (9-10 days per chapter followed by chapter test)

SEMESTER I

Demo: Capítulo 2: *Después de clase*

Day 1
<u>Objectives</u>: Introduce the concept of time, schedules and leisure activities and places
<u>Topics</u>: Tema 1 Vocabulario, Gramática 1
<u>Materials</u>: Textbook, pictures/ props, video

Activity	Time allotted for activity	Class Activity	Textbook activities
1	15 Minutes	- Greet students and ask them how they are doing in Spanish. -<u>Introduction to the chapter.</u> Present the chapter theme and review the cultural information presented in the chapter opener. - <u>Introduction to the Vocabulary</u>. Write on the board the following questions: 1. *¿Qué día es hoy?* 2. *¿Qué hora es?* 3. *¿A qué hora es la clase de español?* 4. *¿Qué clases tomas los lunes, miércoles y viernes a las diez de la mañana?* 5. *¿Qué haces (what do you do) los viernes por la noche?* - <u>Objectives</u>: Introduce the 2 main points of today's class and its objectives, as stated on the syllabus then, proceed to answer the first question *Hoy es lunes 5 de octubre, 2009.* Mention that the Spanish calendar starts with Monday and ends with Sunday, and that the days of the week and the months of the year are not capitalized in Spanish, as they are in English.	***Una conversación,* 2-1 to 2-3**

Activity	Time allotted for activity	Class Activity	Textbook activities
1		- <u>Oral & Written Practice</u>: Activity *Una conversación* and 2-3 *Otra conversacíon*. Because of time constraints, the instructor may want to mention in the previous class that *Una conversación* should be studied before coming to class, therefore, the new vocabulary and grammatical structures are clear.	
2	10 Minutes	- Explain the use of the definite article *el* or *los* in front of the days of the week *(el/ los lunes)* to refer to repetitive actions on certain days. <u>Oral & Written Practice</u>: Use different clocks/ watches at different times (these could be toys or pictures). Ask students to tell the time, by using *y (cuarto) and menos (cuarto)* for the minutes. - Explain that time is femenine in Spanish and the reason why we use *la una y las dos…* - Clarify the difference between "what time is it?" and "at what time does an activity take place?"	**2-4 to 2-5**
3	10 Minutes	<u>Communicative Exercise</u>: You may consider using the Supplemental activity on p. 38, so students can practice the days of the week: Distribute copies of daily planners for a week and ask students to take turns describing their class and work schedules using different times and days of the week. In addition to producing complete sentences, pay attention to students' pronunciation of *miércoles* and *sábado* where the accent is usually misplaced.	
4	5 Minutes	<u>Assessment on written exercises</u>: Correct the assigned written activities on the syllabus, and collect the assignments.	
5	5 Minutes	- **Option 1.** <u>Listening Comprehension</u>: Assign ¡*A escuchar*! (CD 1 Track 27), with books closed then, with books opened to assess students' listening and	*¡A escuchar!*

Activity	Time allotted for activity	Class Activity	Textbook activities
5		comprehension skills. - **Option 2** <u>Communicative Exercise</u>: Correct Activity 2-6 *Entrevista* This pair activity will be practiced in class orally. The instructor may collect the written version of this activity assignment to assess the proper use of *gustar* verb. *If time does not allow, the instructor may well consider starting the next class with the *Entrevista* activity.	**2-6**
6	5 Minutes	- <u>Final Summary</u>: Review the *¡Ojo!* box and do 2-7 *Comparaciones culturales* to practice converting from a 24-hour clock to a 12-hour clock. Review the new concepts of time, days of the week, and leisure activities and places that are written on the board. Ask students if they are clear and if they have any questions. - Ask students to review the self-check questions in *Para averiguar* or you may wish to use them to quickly check that students have understood the explanations. Repeat selected expressions and correct their pronunciation. - Take-leave in Spanish, and remind them to follow the instructions on the syllabus, and have their assignments completed before coming to class.	**2-7**

<u>Homework:</u>

1. Instructors may remind their students that they should plan on studying at least two hours for every hour in class. Students may be advised that they are expected to do all the activities before coming to class, as stated earlier on the syllabus.

2. Instructors may also advise their students to follow up with the contents and requirements of the syllabus, as stated for each day of the week.

3. Do SAM 2-1 to 2-9

<u>Objectives</u>: Locate people and places using the verb *estar* and adverbs of frequency; exchange information about leisure time and daily activities in the Hispanic world
<u>Topics</u>: Tema 1 Gramática 2; Tema 2 Vocabulario
<u>Materials</u>: Textbook, pictures/ props, video

Online	My Spanish Lab (MSL) Textbook Activities
15 Minutes - Have students consider the following questions before reading *Gramática 2* about the verb *estar*: 1. *¿Cómo estás?* 2. *¿Dónde estás ahora?* 3. *¿Estás en clase todos los días?* - Students should review the self-check questions in *Para averiguar* before proceeding to the activities. - <u>Written Practice</u>: Have students complete 2-8 to 2-10. They should practice answering the questions aloud in 2-10 as they may be asked to practice with a partner in class.	2-8 to 2-10
15 Minutes <u>Introduction to Vocabulary</u>: *Las actividades diarias* - Have students listen to the audio program (CD 1, Track 28) for *Las actividades diarias* and *Una conversación* (CD 1, Track 29). <u>Listening comprehension practice</u> Ask students to answer the following questions as they listen to *Una conversación* a second time: 1. *Generalmente, ¿Cómo está Diego los viernes por la noche?* 2. *¿Qué le gusta hacer los viernes por la noche?* - <u>Written Practice</u>: Complete 2-11 to 2-12 and prepare 2-13 *Otra conversación* to complete with a partner for the next class or they can practice with an online partner.	**2-11 to 2-12**
10 Minutes - <u>Listening comprehension practice</u>: *¡A escuchar!* (CD 1, Track 30) -Then have students prepare 2-13 *Otra conversación* to complete	***¡A escuchar!* and 2-13**

Online	My Spanish Lab (MSL) Textbook Activities
with a partner in the next class or they can practice with an online partner.	
10 Minutes - <u>Final Summary</u>: Review the verb *estar,* locations and adverbs of frequency. Encourage students to prepare and/or post any questions they may have pertaining to the material presented.	

Homework:
1. Do SAM 2-10 to 2-18

Day 3

<u>Objectives</u>: Introduce the **–ar** verbs in the present tense; ask and answer questions, and talk about your activities

<u>Topics</u>: Tema 2 Gramática 2

<u>Materials</u>: Textbook, pictures/ props, video

Activity	Time allotted for activity	Class Activity	Textbook activities
1	15 Minutes	- Write on the board the following questions: 1. *¿Cocinas todos los días? 2. ¿Con qué frecuencia miras la televisión? 3. ¿Estudias más en casa o en la biblioteca?* - Greet students and ask them if they have any questions. You may also want to allow students time to practice 2-12 *¿Y tú?* or 2-13 *Otra conversación* with a partner. - <u>Objectives</u>: Introduce the main points of today's class and its objectives, as stated on the syllabus then, proceed to answer the questions 1. *"Sí, cocino todos los días"*, 2. *"Miro la televisión todas las tardes"*, 3. *No, estudio más en la biblioteca"*. - <u>Introduction to *Gramática 1*</u>. The (-ar) verbs in the present tense. Clarify that the Spanish verbs are classified in 3 categories (-ar), (-er), and (-ir) verbs. - Go over the verb conjugation with all the subject pronouns and introduce the other verbs from the list in context (p. 44). Also clarify the difference between the affirmative and the negative forms. - <u>Oral & Written Practice</u>: You may assign 2-14 to 2-16 (if time allows).	**2-14 to 2-16**
2	15 Minutes	- Introduce Question Formation in Spanish. Explain the different ways Spanish-speaking people ask questions: 1. By raising their intonation in a statement, 2. By switching the order of the verb-subject, 3. By using a tag question, 4. By using interrogative words	

Activity	Time allotted for activity	Class Activity	Textbook activities
2		- <u>Oral & Written Practice</u>: You may consider using the Supplemental Activity on p. 46.	**2-17 to 2-19**
3	10 minutes	- <u>Instructor's Assessment on Communicative and Written Exercises</u>: Correct individually the assigned oral/ written activities and collect the assignments ** It should be stated previously on the syllabus that the instructor may/ may not collect the assigned homework, and may/ may not announce a quiz.	
4	10 minutes	- <u>Final Summary</u>: Go over the (-ar) verbs in the present tense, and the Question Formation. Ask students if they are clear and if they have any questions. - Ask students to review the self-check questions in *Para averiguar* or you may wish to use them to quickly check that students have understood the explanations. - Take-leave in Spanish, and remind them to follow the instructions on the syllabus, and have their assignments completed before coming to class.	

<u>Homework</u>:
1. Do SAM 2-19 to 2-27

Objectives: Indicating locations close to the university and use of prepositions of place and contractions with **de**
Topics: Tema 3 Vocabulario, Gramática 1
Materials: Textbook, pictures/ props, video

Online	MSL Textbook Activities
20 Minutes - Introduction to Vocabulary: *Lugares cerca de la universidad* - Have students consider the following questions as they review the illustrations: *"¿Qué hay en tu ciudad?, ¿Qué lugares hay para divertirse? (have fun)"* - Have students listen to the audio program (CD 1, Track 31) for *Lugares cerca de la universidad* and *Una conversación* (CD 1, Track 32). Listening Comprehension Practice -Ask students to answer the following questions as they listen to *Una conversación* a second time: 1. *¿Dónde prefiere estudiar Inés?* 2. *¿Le gusta estudiar por la tarde o por la noche?* - You may assign *¡A escuchar!* (CD 1, Track 33) Written Practice: Complete 2-20 to 2-22 and prepare 2-23 *Otra conversación* to complete with a partner for the next class or they can practice with an online partner.	*Una conversación* **2-20 to 2-23**
20 Minutes - Read *Gramática 1* about prepositions of place and contractions with *de.* Go over the list of prepositions, and the use of *de, del* (+ masculine singular noun), and *de la* (+feminine singular noun) -Students should review the self-check questions in *Para averiguar* before proceeding to the activities. - Written Practice: 2-24 to 2-25 and 2-27	**2-24 to 2-25, 2-27**

Online	MSL Textbook Activities
10 Minutes - <u>Final Summary</u>: Review the new vocabulary and the prepositions of place and contractions with *de.* Encourage students to prepare and/or post any questions they may have pertaining to the material presented. - Prepare 2-26 to practice the next day in class. Sketch the street and label each of the buildings using the names from the list.	**2-26**

<u>Homework</u>:
1. Do SAM 2-28 to 2-33

Day 5

<u>Objectives</u>: Saying what you are going to do, using the verb "***ir***" and "***ir***" a + infinitive, contractions with ***a***, and Los pasatiempos;

<u>Topics</u>: Tema 3 Gramática 2, Tema 4 Vocabulario

<u>Materials</u>: Textbook, pictures/ props, video

Activity	Time allotted for activity	Class Activity	Textbook activities
1	15minutes	- <u>Objectives</u>: Introduce the verb *ir* in context of locations and its use to indicate "near future", as stated on the syllabus. - Greet students and ask them if they have any questions. Do a quick comprehension check using 2-25 to assess whether students have understood the material. You may also want to allow students time to practice 2-26 with a partner. - <u>Conjugation of the verb *Ir* in the present tense</u>. Indicate its irregular nature as a verb. - Talk about things that are going to happen in the near future, by using *ir a* + infinitive and adverbs of time *esta tarde", "la semana que viene".* - Ask students about their plans next weekend: where they are going, and what they are going to do. Write on the board their answers, and make sure that their pronunciation and grammatical structures are correct.	**2-28 to 2-32**
2	15 minutes	- <u>Introduce Vocabulary</u>: *Los pasatiempos* Review the (-ar) verbs, the verb *ir* and locations, while introducing hobbies and leisure activities. - <u>Listening Comprehension Practice</u>: You may assign *Una conversación* (CD 1, Track 35). As suggested, have students listen and comprehend the conversation first with their books closed, then allow them to open their books and look for the correct answers. Then, *¡A escuchar!,*(CD 1, Track 36)	**2-33 to 2-34** ***Una conversación*, ¡A escuchar!**
3	10 minutes	- <u>Communicative Exercise</u>	**2-35**

Activity	Time allotted for activity	Class Activity	Textbook activities
3		-Assign 2-35 *Otra conversación* and have students practice with a partner. You may have pairs present their conversations for the class.	
4	10 minutes	- <u>Final Summary</u>: Go over the verb *ir,* the new vocabulary, and the reading(s). Ask students if they are clear and if they have any questions. -Ask students to review the self-check questions in *Para averiguar* or you may wish to use them to quickly check that students have understood the explanations. - Take-leave in Spanish, and remind them to follow the instructions on the syllabus, and have their assignments completed before coming to class.	

<u>Homework</u>:
1. Do SAM 2-34 to 2-40

<u>Objectives</u>: Chapter review using real-life simulation of working in the Hispanic Chamber of Commerce, Cultural reading
<u>Topics</u>: Tema 4 Resumen de gramática, *En la vida real* and Hoy día *Lectores de hoy*
<u>Materials</u>: Textbook, pictures/ props, video

Online	MSL Textbook Activities
20 Minutes -Have students read through *Resumen de gramática* and complete the activities for *En la vida real* to review chapter grammar in real-life simulation of working in the Hispanic Chamber of Commerce. - Practice activity 2-39 *¿Y tú?* and 2-42 with your online partner and/or prepare to practice in class with a partner. -Encourage students to visit MySpanishLab for more *Entre profesionales* vocabulary and activities related to professions and careers.	**2-37 to 2-42, *Entre profesionales***
20 Minutes -Read *Lectores de hoy, Moda global* in the *Hoy día* section. Encourage students to review the reading strategy before proceeding to the reading. Have students complete the activities in *Antes de leer, Ahora tú* and *Después de leer.*	**2-43 to 2-47**
10 Minutes - <u>Final Summary</u>: Review assignments and prepare the paired activities to be practiced in class. Review the main message of the reading to discuss in class. - Encourage students to prepare and/or post any questions they may have pertaining to the material presented.	

<u>Homework:</u>
1. Do SAM 2-53 to 2-55

Day 7

<u>Objectives</u>: Cultural contact: listening , viewing, speaking and writing
<u>Topics</u>: Voces de la calle and Escritores en acción
<u>Materials</u>: Textbook, pictures/ props, video

Activity	Time allotted for activity	Class Activity	Textbook activities
1	10 minutes	- Greet students and ask them how they are doing in Spanish. Do a quick warm-up with 2-42 *Mi restaurante favorite*. You may also want to allow students time to practice 2-26 with a partner. - <u>Objectives</u>: Cultural contact: listening , viewing, speaking and writing about social, artistic and political projects where students can participate in, and make a difference in their own community and society	
2	15 minutes	- **Option 1**. -<u>Introduce</u> *Voces de la calle: Centros sociales comunitarios* - Make a link between the verb *ir* and its use in the near future and the cultural component about civic engagement, and ask students to predict one social commitment -You can have students view the video in class or assign for homework. - **Option 2**. -<u>Introduce</u> *Escritores en acción: Tu perfil en internet* You may use the writing strategies, as suggested, in order to invite students to think and to write about their personal profile in myspace.latino. This is an engaging activity that aims at reviewing the new vocabulary of schedules, hobbies and leisure, the (-ar) verbs, the verb *gustar,* the verb *ir,* the verb *estar* and locations, and other relevant information of self description and qualities.	2-48 to 2-51 2-52 to 2-56

Activity	Time allotted for activity	Class Activity	Textbook activities
2		- At the end, students may exchange their creative work with other students and with their instructor, for constructive feedback and evaluation of content, style and creativity	
3	15 minutes	<u>Sample Exam.</u> As an effective practice, instructors may consider giving their students an exam (from the exam bank) which contemplates reading, writing, and listening skills. This is a good practice before the chapter exam	
4	5 minutes	- <u>Final Summary</u>: Review the main components of chapter 2. Ask students if they are clear and if they have any questions. - Take-leave in Spanish, and remind them to study for the exam the next class day.	

<u>Homework</u>:
1. Do SAM 2- 56 to 2-58

Objectives: General review of the vocabulary, grammar and culture of Chapter 2 (ON LINE, this will be a second chance for students who may need further assistance)
Topics: Tema 1-Tema 4; Resumen de Gramática, Vocabulario
Materials: Textbook, pictures/ props, video

Online	MSL Textbook Activities
Prepare students for Chapter 2 Exam: *Después de clase* -Review grammar in *Resumen de gramática* and be certain that all verb conjugations and sentence structures are clear. -Review vocabulary using the end vocabulary list and ask students to use the new words and expressions properly in complete and coherent sentences or paragraphs. Encourage students to visit the Mnemonic Dictionary online as an additional study aid. -Encourage students to use this time to explore the interactive travelogue, *Escapadas,* in MySpanishLab or it may be assigned for homework.	**Mnemonic dictionary, MySpanishLab**

Homework:
1. Do SAM 2- 41 to 2-51

Day 9

<u>Objectives</u>: Assessment of chapter vocabulary, grammar and culture
<u>Topics</u>: *Capítulo 2* Test
<u>Materials</u>: Test

Activity	Time allotted for activity	Class Activity	Textbook activities
1	5 minutes	- Greet students and do a quick review using questions from the *Para averiguar* boxes.	
2	40 minutes	*Capítulo 2* Test	
3	5 minutes	-<u>Introduction to *Capítulo 3*</u>. Use the last few minutes of class to present the chapter theme and review the cultural information presented in the chapter opener.	

<u>Homework</u>:
1. Review cultural information presented in chapter opener of *Capítulo 3*, p. 67
2. Do SAM 3-1 to 3-4

2 Después de clase

Tema 1: ¿Qué día? ¿A qué hora?

Vocabulario: Mi horario

2-1 ▶ El horario de Miguel. Read Miguel's schedule, and match the following statements based on the information given.

	lunes	martes	miércoles	jueves	viernes	sábado	domingo
9:00–10:00	español		español		español		
10:00–11:00	informática	biología	informática	biología	informática		
11:00-12:00	laboratorio		laboratorio		laboratorio		
12:00–1:00	cafetería	arte	cafetería	arte	cafetería		
1:00–2:00							
2:00–3:00	biblioteca	tenis	biblioteca	tenis		fútbol	
3:00–4:00	biblioteca		biblioteca				
4:00–5:00	biblioteca		biblioteca		¡FIESTA!		

1. Los lunes, miércoles y viernes, a las 9 de la mañana, _____

2. Después de la clase de biología, _____

3. Los lunes de dos a cinco, _____

4. Los sábados a las dos de la tarde, _____

5. Los miércoles al mediodía, _____

6. Los martes y jueves por la tarde, _____

a. Miguel está en la cafetería con sus amigos.

b. Miguel practica tenis.

c. Miguel estudia en la biblioteca.

d. Miguel tiene clase de español.

e. Miguel no tiene clase.

f. Miguel practica fútbol.

2-2 ▶ Una conversación. Complete the following telephone conversation between Ángela and Patricio using the words from the list.

juntos	fin de semana	de	trabajo	sola	conmigo	estoy

ÁNGELA: Hola, Patricio. ¿Cómo estás?

PATRICIO: Muy bien. ¿Y tú?

ÁNGELA: Muy bien. (1) _____ en la cafetería con Ana y Raquel. ¿Dónde estás tú?

PATRICIO: Estoy en la biblioteca porque tengo un examen de matemáticas esta semana.

ÁNGELA: No me gusta estudiar (2) _____. ¿Te gustaría estudiar (3)

_____ este (4) _____ o trabajas el sábado y el domingo?

PATRICIO: Sí, (5) _____ el sábado de 9 a 3 y el domingo

(6) _____ 9 a 12, pero casi siempre estoy en la biblioteca los domingos

después del trabajo y me gustaría estudiar (7) _____.

ÁNGELA: Perfecto. ¿A qué hora?

PATRICIO: ¿A las dos?

ÁNGELA: ¡Muy bien! Hasta el domingo.

2-3 ▶ ¿Dónde está Ramón? The following drawings show you a typical day for Ramón. Complete the sentences by telling where Ramón is at each time of day. Choose among the following possibilities.

| en casa | en el trabajo | en el autobús |

Modelo: A las siete de la mañana, Ramón está *en casa.*

1. A las ocho y veinte de la mañana, Ramón está _____.

2. A las nueve menos veinte de la mañana, Ramón está _____.

3. A las nueve y media de la mañana, Ramón está _____.

4. A las seis de la tarde, Ramón está _____.

2-4 ▶ Tu horario. Answer the questions you hear about your schedule, and be sure to write out the hours in words.

Modelo: ¿Dónde estás los miércoles a las diez y media de la mañana?
A las diez y media de la mañana, estoy en clase de historia.

1. _____

2. _____

3. _____

4. _____

5. _____

Gramática 1: *Describing your schedule: Time and days of the week*
(TEXTBOOK P. 38)

2-5 ▶ ¿Qué hora es? Look at each clock, and write what time it is. Be sure to write a complete sentence giving the time, using **es or son,** and also tell whether it is morning, afternoon, or night.

Modelo:

Son las dos y media de la tarde.

1.

2.

3.

1. _____.

2. _____.

3. _____.

4.

5.

6.

4. _____.

5. _____.

6. _____.

2-6 ▶ El programa de televisión. Look at the schedule of the following television programs from Spain and complete the sentences, following the model.

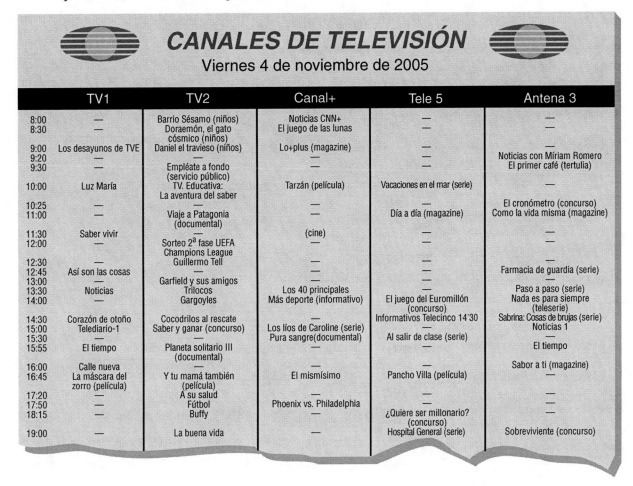

CANALES DE TELEVISIÓN
Viernes 4 de noviembre de 2005

	TV1	TV2	Canal+	Tele 5	Antena 3
8:00	—	Barrio Sésamo (niños)	Noticias CNN+	—	—
8:30	—	Doraemón, el gato cósmico (niños)	El juego de las lunas	—	—
9:00	Los desayunos de TVE	Daniel el travieso (niños)	Lo+plus (magazine)	—	Noticias con Míriam Romero
9:20	—		—	—	El primer café (tertulia)
9:30	—	Empléate a fondo (servicio público)	—	—	
10:00	Luz María	TV. Educativa: La aventura del saber	Tarzán (película)	Vacaciones en el mar (serie)	
10:25	—		—		El cronómetro (concurso)
11:00	—	Viaje a Patagonia (documental)	—	Día a día (magazine)	Como la vida misma (magazine)
11:30	Saber vivir		(cine)	—	—
12:00	—	Sorteo 2ª fase UEFA Champions League	—	—	—
12:30	—	Guillermo Tell	—	—	—
12:45	Así son las cosas		—	—	Farmacia de guardia (serie)
13:00	—	Garfield y sus amigos	—	—	Paso a paso (serie)
13:30	Noticias	Trilocos	Los 40 principales	El juego del Euromillón (concurso)	Nada es para siempre (teleserie)
14:00	—	Gargoyles	Más deporte (informativo)	Informativos Telecinco 14'30	Sabrina: Cosas de brujas (serie)
14:30	Corazón de otoño	Cocodrilos al rescate			Noticias 1
15:00	Telediario-1	Saber y ganar (concurso)	Los líos de Caroline (serie)	Al salir de clase (serie)	
15:30	—		Pura sangre(documental)		El tiempo
15:55	El tiempo	Planeta solitario III (documental)	—		
16:00	Calle nueva		—	Pancho Villa (película)	Sabor a ti (magazine)
16:45	La máscara del zorro (película)	Y tu mamá también (película)	El mismísimo		—
17:20	—	A su salud	—	—	—
17:50	—	Fútbol	Phoenix vs. Philadelphia	—	—
18:15	—	Buffy	—	¿Quiere ser millonario? (concurso)	—
19:00	—	La buena vida	—	Hospital General (serie)	Sobreviviente (concurso)

tres y media	*antes de*	después de	hasta	antes de	de a

Modelo: Los "40 principales" es *antes de* "Más deporte".

1. "Al salir de clase" es a las _____ de la tarde en Tele 5.

2. "Cocodrilos al rescate" es _____ "Saber y ganar".

3. "La máscara del zorro" es _____ "Calle nueva".

4. "Corazón de otoño" es de las dos y media de la tarde _____ las tres.

5. "Sabrina: cosas de brujas" es _____ 2:30 _____ 3:00.

2-7 ▶ La semana de Emma. Emma likes to be very busy during the week. Complete the description of her activities by writing out in letters the time that you see in parentheses.

Modelo: Los lunes tengo clase de español a las *nueve* (9:00).

1. Los martes, estudio con mis amigas en la biblioteca al _____ (noon).

2. Los fines de semana, desayuno (*I have breakfast*) a las _____ (10:30).

3. Los viernes, estoy en la cafetería a la _____ (12:45).

4. Los miércoles, tengo clase de química a las _____ (8:30).

5. Todos los días de la semana, trabajo a las _____ (6:40).

2-8 ▶ Los días de la semana. Complete the sentences logically with the missing days of the week.

1. El día después de martes es _____.

2. El Día de Acción de Gracias (*Thanksgiving*) es siempre un _____.

3. El primer día de la semana laboral (*work week*) es _____.

4. Los días del fin de semana son sábado y _____.

5. El día antes de sábado es _____.

2-9 ▶ Unas preguntas. Answer the questions you hear in complete sentences.

Modelo: ¿Qué días de la semana trabajas?
           Trabajo los lunes, miércoles y jueves.

1. _____

2. _____

3. _____

4. _____

5. _____

Gramática 2: *Saying where you are: The verb **estar*** (TEXTBOOK P. 40)

2-10 ▶ ¿Vamos a comer? Ana and Emilio haven't seen each other during the whole summer, and want to make plans. Complete their phone conversation with the correct forms of the verb **estar**.

ANA: Hola, Emilio, soy Ana. ¿Cómo (1) _____?

EMILIO: (2) _____ muy bien. ¿Y tú?

ANA: Muy bien también. ¿Dónde (3) _____ ahora?

EMILIO: (4) _____ en un café. Mis amigos Laura y Juan (5) _____

conmigo. Y tú, ¿dónde (6) _____?

ANA: Mi compañera de cuarto y yo (7) _____ en la biblioteca, pero

_____ (8) cansadas de estudiar. ¿En qué café (9) _____

ustedes?

EMILIO: (10) _____ en el café Acapulco. ¿Te gustaría venir (*to come*)?

ANA: Sí. ¡Nos vemos en quince minutos!

2-11 ▶ ¿Dónde estás? Answer the following questions about yourself, your friends, and your family. You can use **No sé dónde está(n)** if you do not know where people are on certain days.

Modelo: ¿Generalmente, dónde estás los lunes a las tres de la tarde?
Generalmente, los lunes a las tres de la tarde estoy en clase.

1. ¿Generalmente, dónde estás los sábados por la mañana?

_____

2. ¿Dónde estás ahora?

_____

3. ¿Generalmente, dónde están tus amigos el jueves por la tarde?

_____

4. ¿Dónde está tu profesor/a de español los lunes por la mañana?

_____

5. ¿Qué días están ustedes en la clase de español?

_____

2-12 ▶ ¿Con qué frecuencia? Listen to Celia as she talks about her activities during the week, and complete the following sentences with the correct phrase to indicate frequency.

1. Celia está en el gimnasio [con frecuencia / una vez a la semana].

2. Tiene clase de español [tres veces a la semana / todos los días].

3. Está con su (*her*) familia [los fines de semana / todos los días].

4. Estudia con sus amigos en la biblioteca [a veces / todos los días].

5. Los martes Celia tiene clase [a veces / todo el día].

2-13 ▶ ¿Y tú? Complete the following sentences with information about the frequency of your activities.

1. ¿Con qué frecuencia estás en la biblioteca?

_____

2. ¿Con qué frecuencia estás en la cafetería de la universidad?

_____

3. ¿Con qué frecuencia estás en la clase de español?

_____

4. ¿Con qué frecuencia estás en el gimnasio?

_____

5. ¿Con qué frecuencia estás en casa con tu familia?

_____

2-14 ▶ Tu semana. Describe your weekly schedule orally. Be sure to mention your classes, when you study and work, and when you are with friends.

Tema 2: ¿Qué te gusta hacer después de clase?

Vocabulario: Las actividades diarias

2-15 ▶ ¿Qué hacen? During the weekend, Ana and her friends do many leisure activities. Match the following images with the activities that they illustrate.

1. _____

2. _____

3. _____

4. _____

a. bailar en una discoteca

b. trabajar en el jardín (*garden*)

c. mirar la televisión

d. tomar algo con unos amigos

e. hablar por teléfono

f. comprar ropa

5. _____

6. _____

2-16 ▶ Las actividades. Match each verb with the most logical word or expression.

1. _____ escuchar

2. _____ comer

3. _____ bailar

4. _____ mirar

5. _____ hablar

6. _____ estudiar

a. la televisión

b. en una discoteca

c. por teléfono

d. la radio

e. química en la biblioteca

f. en un restaurante

2-17 ▶ El fin de semana de Juan y Pedro. The following are the activities that Juan and Pedro do during the weekend. Select the activity in each group that does not belong.

1. a. ir al cine   b. bailar   c. salir   d. trabajar

2. a. tocar la guitarra   b. escuchar música   c. cantar   d. cocinar

3. a. preparar la cena   b. limpiar   c. bailar   d. cocinar

4. a. bailar   b. trabajar en la oficina c. cantar   d. escuchar música

2-18 ▶ ¿Y tú? Answer the questions you hear about your own activities, and those of your friends and family. Remember to write complete sentences.

1. _____

2. _____

3. _____

4. _____

5. _____

Gramática 1: *Talking about your activities: Regular –ar verbs*
(TEXTBOOK P. 44)

2-19 ▶ Los sujetos. Select the subject(s) that can be used with the following conjugated verbs. There might be more than one correct answer for each.

1. limpian
   a. yo   b. nosotros   c. ustedes   d. ellos

2. llegamos
   a. nosotros   b. ustedes   c. usted   d. Iván y yo

3. compras
   a. ustedes   b. ellas   c. tú   d. Jesús y José

4. canto
   a. Pablo   b. tú   c. yo   d. usted

5. escucha
   a. Marcos   b. mi amiga   c. usted   d. ustedes

6. descansan
   a. nosotros   b. tú   c. ellas   d. Lucía

2-20 ▶ ¿Qué hacen? Marco knows a lot of people on campus and he tells his new roommate what they do during the week. Complete the following sentences with the correct form of the appropriate verbs from the list.

estudiar	bailar	hablar	preparar	llegar	mirar	tocar

Modelo: Nosotros *estudiamos* mucho después de las clases.

1. Juana _____ en la discoteca.

2. Carolina y Victoria _____ a casa a las ocho de la noche.

3. Elena y yo _____ por teléfono todos los días.

4. Verónica y sus padres _____ la televisión los sábados por la noche.

5. Patricia y María _____ la cena para sus (*their*) amigos.

6. Tú _____ música con tu banda.

2-21 ▶ Después de clase. Andrés and Diego are talking about their activities after class. Based on the conversation you hear, decide whether each of the following statements is **cierto** (true) or **falso** (false). Select **No se menciona** if it is not mentioned.

1. Diego está muy ocupado.	Cierto	Falso	No se menciona.
2. Andrés está cansado.	Cierto	Falso	No se menciona.
3. Después de clase, Diego trabaja hasta las siete.	Cierto	Falso	No se menciona.
4. Después de ir a la biblioteca, Andrés tiene una clase.	Cierto	Falso	No se menciona.
5. Diego necesita limpiar su cuarto mañana.	Cierto	Falso	No se menciona.
6. El domingo, hay un concierto.	Cierto	Falso	No se menciona.

Gramática 2: *Asking questions: Question formation* (TEXTBOOK P. 46)

2-22 ▶ ¿Verdad? Lucía is not sure that she heard what her friend Enrique told her, and she wants to make sure she understood it all. Unscramble each group of words to form "yes" or "no" questions, and be sure to begin with the capitalized word. Also remember to include a comma in your answer, as in the model.

Modelo: ¿verdad? / Te gusta / con frecuencia / al cine / ir
         Te gusta ir al cine con frecuencia, ¿verdad?

1. las siete / ¿verdad? / a / Trabajas

   _____

2. en la biblioteca / esta tarde / Estudias / ¿no?

   _____

3. tus compañeros de cuarto / ¿verdad? / con / Cocinas

   _____

4. tus padres (*parents*) / por teléfono / Hablas / ¿verdad? / con

   _____

5. la televisión / ¿no? / por la noche / Miras

   _____

2-23 ▶ Unas preguntas. Paula and Cecilia meet for the first time in French class. Match Cecilia's questions with Paula's responses.

Cecilia:

1. ¿De dónde eres? _____

2. ¿Dónde trabajas? _____

3. ¿Por qué estudias francés? _____

4. ¿Cuál es tu clase favorita? _____

5. ¿Dónde estudias? _____

6. ¿Con qué frecuencia hablas con tus padres? _____

Paula:

a. Trabajo en un restaurante mexicano.

b. Estudio en la biblioteca.

c. Porque me gustan las lenguas.

d. Soy de Buenos Aires.

e. Dos veces a la semana.

f. Es la clase de biología.

2-24 ▶ Tu nuevo compañero de cuarto. Felipe has a new roommate, Pedro, and they meet on the first day of the semester. Complete the questions Pedro asks Felipe with the interrogative words from the list.

De dónde	Qué	Quién	Cómo	Cuántas	Cuál

1. — ¿ _____ te llamas?
   — Me llamo Felipe.

2. — ¿ _____ eres?
   — Soy de México.

3. — ¿ _____ estudias?
   — Estudio lenguas.

4. — ¿ _____ clases tienes este semestre?
   — Tengo cuatro clases este semestre.

5. — ¿ _____ es tu profesor/a favorito/a?
   — Mi profesor favorito es el Señor Leblanc, mi profesor de francés.

6. — ¿ _____ es tu clase favorita?
   — Mi clase favorita es la clase de francés.

2-25 ▶ ¿Y tú? Listen to the following questions a new friend asks about your own life, and answer in complete sentences.

1. _____

2. _____

3. _____

4. _____

5. _____

6. _____

2-26 ▶ ¿Qué o cuál? Complete each question with either **qué** or **cuál,** as appropriate.

1. ¿(Qué / Cuál) es tu clase más difícil?

2. ¿(Qué / Cuál) es un sustantivo?

3. ¿(Qué / Cuál) te gusta hacer los fines de semana?

4. ¿(Qué / Cuál) es el mejor restaurante de la ciudad?

5. ¿(Qué / Cuál) haces durante las vacaciones?

6. ¿(Qué / Cuál) es tu libro favorito?

2-27 ▶ Diario. Write an e-mail to a friend explaining what you do during the week after classes and how you spend your weekends. Then ask at least three questions about his / her activities. Use the **-ar** verbs presented in this *Tema,* and use verbs like **comer** (*to eat*), **ir** (*to go*) or **salir** (*to go out*) in the infinitive after **me / te gusta** to talk about what you like to do.

_____

_____

_____

_____

_____

Tema 3: ¿Adónde vas?

Vocabulario: Lugares cerca de la universidad

2-28 ▶ Cerca de la universidad. Match the following activities with the places where they most logically occur.

1. comprar un libro _____   a. en el cine

2. hacer ejercicio _____   b. en un club nocturno

3. bailar _____   c. en un centro comercial

4. ver una película _____   d. en el gimnasio

5. ver un partido de fútbol _____   e. en la librería

6. comprar ropa _____   f. en el estadio

2-29 ▶ ¿Dónde están? Elena and her friends are spending their time after class in different ways. Look at the drawings and complete the sentences to tell where they are.

Modelo:

Ramón está *en el supermercado*.

1. María está _____.   2. Amanda está _____.

3. Laura y Daniel están

_____.

4. Víctor y Catalina están

_____.

5. Marcos, Ana y Diego están

_____.

2-30 ¿Qué hacemos esta noche? Complete the following conversation between Antonio and Juan with the appropriate words or phrases from the list.

lado	calle	fútbol americano	abierto
restaurante	cerca	lugar	estadio

ANTONIO: Hola, Juan. ¿Te gustaría ir a comer juntos esta noche?

JUAN: Qué buena idea. ¿Adónde quieres ir?

ANTONIO: ¿Qué te parece el (1) _____ mexicano (2) _____ de la

universidad? Está en la (3) _____ Martínez.

JUAN: Es el restaurante nuevo al (4) _____ de la biblioteca, ¿verdad?

ANTONIO: Sí, es un (5) _____ muy bonito.

JUAN: ¿Está (6) _____ los lunes?

ANTONIO: Creo que los domingos está cerrado, pero los otros días de la semana está abierto. ¿Te gusta
la comida mexicana?

JUAN: Sí, mucho. ¿Y después, te gustaría ir al (7) _____ a ver el partido de

(8) _____?

ANTONIO: Me parece muy bien. ¿Nos vemos a las seis?

JUAN: Perfecto. Hasta luego.

Gramática 1: *Indicating location: Prepositions of place and contractions with* **de** (Textbook p. 50)

2-31 ▶ La universidad. Some high school students are visiting your university campus and need help
finding different buildings. Answer their questions based on the campus map provided, and be sure to use
a different preposition in each answer.

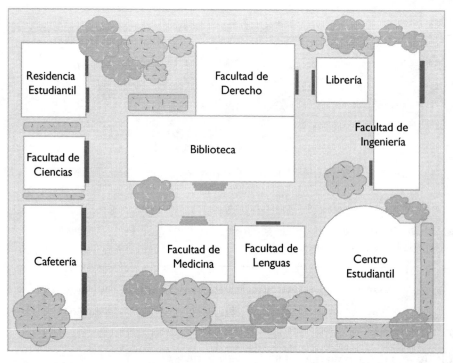

Modelo: ¿Dónde está la Facultad de Derecho?
         Está a la izquierda de la librería.

1. ¿Dónde está la Facultad de Ingeniería?

_____

2. ¿Dónde está la Facultad de Medicina?

_____

3. ¿Dónde está la cafetería?

_____

4. ¿Dónde está la biblioteca?

_____

5. ¿Dónde está el centro estudiantil?

_____

2-32 ▶ ¿Cierto o Falso? Marcos is a new student and does not know the university campus very well. Listen to the following statements he makes about the location of the different buildings on his campus, and decide whether they are **cierto** or **falso** based on the map below.

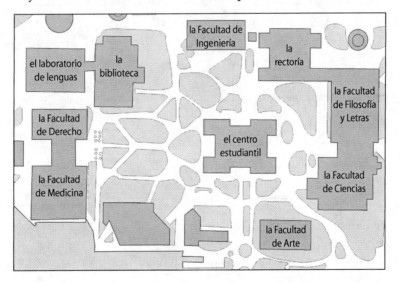

1. Cierto	Falso		5. Cierto	Falso
2. Cierto	Falso		6. Cierto	Falso
3. Cierto	Falso		7. Cierto	Falso
4. Cierto	Falso		8. Cierto	Falso

Nombre: _____ Fecha: _____

2-33 ▶ ¿Dónde está? Look at the drawing of Arturo's room and fill in the blanks with the most appropriate words or phrases from the list.

en	a la izquierda de	enfrente de
debajo de	encima del	entre

Modelo: La computadora está *encima de* la mesa.

1. El televisor está _____ la cama.

2. Los libros están _____ estante.

3. La alfombra (*rug*) está _____ la cama.

4. La cómoda (*chest of drawers*) está _____ la puerta y la cama.

5. La planta está _____ la lámpara (*lamp*).

6. El gato (*cat*) está _____ la cama.

© 2011 Pearson Education, Inc.

Gramática 2: *Saying what you are going to do:* **Ir,** *contractions with* **a, ir a** + *infinitive* (TEXTBOOK P. 52)

2-34 ▶ ¿Adónde van? Emma and her friends need to go to some specific places. Listen to what they have to do, and complete the following sentences with the correct form of the verb **ir** and the place where each of them has to go.

el gimnasio	**la librería**	**el supermercado**
la biblioteca	**el club nocturno**	**el cine**

Modelo: Ana necesita estudiar para la clase de química.
Ella *va a la biblioteca.*

1. Ella _____.

2. Yo _____.

3. Ellos _____.

4. Nosotros _____.

5. Tú _____, ¿verdad?

2-35 ▶ ¿Qué van a hacer? Listen to the statements about what different people are going to do, and select the appropriate description below.

1. a. Van a salir esta noche.   b. No van a salir esta noche.

2. a. Vamos a estar en la oficina todo el día.   b. No vamos a estar en la oficina todo el día.

3. a. Va a pasar el día en casa.   b. No va a pasar el día en casa.

4. a. Voy a comer en un restaurante.   b. No voy a comer en un restaurante.

5. a. Va a cenar (*have dinner*) solo.   b. No va a cenar solo.

6. a. ¿Vas a ir al gimnasio?   b. ¿Vas a ir al supermercado?

2-36 ▶ Este fin de semana. Discuss orally the things you are going to do this weekend. Remember to use the correct form of the verb **ir a** + infinitive.

Tema 4: ¿Adónde te gusta ir los fines de semana?

Vocabulario: Los pasatiempos

2-37 ► ¿Cómo se sienten? Look at the drawings and choose the correct adjective from the list to express how the people are feeling. Be sure to make the necessary agreements.

enojado/a	nervioso/a	contento/a	aburrido/a	triste

INÉS

MARTA

1. Inés está _____.

2. Marta está _____.

MELISA

JORGE

3. Los estudiantes están

_____.

4. Jorge está _____.

5. Melisa está _____.

2-38 ▶ El fin de semana. Look for the following words related to activities you can do and places you can go during the weekend. Words can be found horizontally or vertically.

A	R	T	B	U	I	S	T	O	C	N
C	M	M	O	N	T	A	Ñ	A	O	L
C	E	R	T	P	I	S	C	I	N	A
I	Z	C	O	M	R	T	I	G	C	G
O	Q	V	I	V	I	R	P	L	I	O
M	U	S	E	O	T	S	L	E	E	T
S	I	N	A	G	O	G	A	S	R	U
E	T	E	A	T	R	O	Y	I	T	B
N	A	C	T	R	I	O	A	A	O	O

iglesia   teatro

montaña   concierto

museo   sinagoga

piscina   mezquita

playa   lago

2-39 ▶ ¿Qué vas a hacer en estos lugares? Fill in the blanks with the activities you are going to do the next time you go to the following places.

Modelo: En la biblioteca voy a *estudiar*.

1. En la piscina voy a _____.

2. En la playa voy a _____.

3. En las montañas voy a _____.

4. En el centro comercial voy a _____.

2-40 ▶ Diario. Imagine that your friend is living abroad for a year in Costa Rica. Write him an e-mail asking about where he goes and what he does with his friends in his free time. Then tell him what you like to do outside of class or work, and say what you are going to do this weekend.

_____

_____

_____

_____

_____

_____

_____

Resumen de gramática (TEXTBOOK P. 56)

2-41 ▶ ¿A qué hora? Miguel does a lot of activities during the week. Answer the following questions telling at what time he does each activity, and be sure to write out the times, as in the model.

Modelo: ¿A qué hora practica Miguel el tenis? (4:00 PM)
Miguel practica el tenis a las cuatro de la tarde.

1. ¿A qué hora va Miguel al trabajo? (8:30 AM)

   _____

2. ¿A qué hora toma Miguel su café (*coffee*)? (10:20 AM)

   _____

3. ¿A qué hora va a comer Miguel con sus colegas? (12:00 PM)

   _____

4. ¿A qué hora regresa Miguel a casa? (4:40 PM)

   _____

5. ¿A qué hora mira Miguel la televisión? (7:00 PM)

   _____

6. ¿A qué hora va Miguel a la cama? (10:15 PM)

   _____

2-42 ▶ ¿Qué hace Marta durante la semana? As you listen to the speaker, complete the following sentences about Marta's activities with the correct words.

Marta es una (1) _____ mexicana. Los lunes, (2) _____ y viernes tiene

clase de español, química y (3) _____. Los (4) _____ y jueves, tiene

clases de (5) _____ e informática. Todos los días come con sus amigas en la cafetería de

la universidad. Los lunes (6) _____ practica el tenis con su mejor amiga, Adriana. Los

jueves y viernes (7) _____ va a la (8) _____ de la universidad. Los (9)

_____ por la mañana va a la biblioteca a estudiar. Los domingos va a la iglesia

(10) _____.

2-43 ▶ ¿Siempre? ¿Nunca? ¿A veces? Now, listen to the speaker again and answer the following questions by selecting the words and phrases from the list.

nunca	cuatro veces al mes	*tres veces a la semana*
todos los días	los sábados	dos veces a la semana

Modelo: ¿Con qué frecuencia tiene clase de español?
          tres veces a la semana

1. ¿Con qué frecuencia tiene clase de inglés?

   _____

2. ¿Con qué frecuencia va a la clase de historia?

   _____

3. ¿Con qué frecuencia va a comer en la cafetería de la universidad?

   _____

4. ¿Cuándo va a la biblioteca?

   _____

5. ¿Con qué frecuencia va a la iglesia?

   _____

2-44 ▶ Las actividades de Laura y sus amigos. Laura and her friends are very busy students. Complete each of the following sentences with the correct form of the appropriate verb.

1. Todos los lunes, Paula y yo _____ (estudiar / bailar) juntos en la biblioteca.

2. A veces Marcos y Luis _____ (rezar / escuchar) música en su apartamento.

3. María _____ (nadar / hablar) por teléfono con sus padres con frecuencia.

4. Yo _____ (cocinar / comprar) todos los días al mediodía en mi casa.

5. Tú _____ (limpiar / cantar) el apartamento una vez a la semana.

6. Penélope y tú _____ (mirar / tomar) la televisión por la noche.

2-45 ▶ ¿Qué van a hacer? Unscramble each group of words telling what the following students are going to do. Remember to use **ir a** + infinitive, as in the model, and to begin each sentence with the proper name(s) or pronoun.

Modelo: salir / Inés y Mario / esta noche
          Inés y Mario van a salir esta noche.

1. en el supermercado / comprar / Ana / comida

   _____.

2. al club nocturno / Juan y yo / bailar

   _____.

3. Lola y Paula / la clase / estudiar / para / de español

   _____.

4. hablar / con tus amigos / Tú / por teléfono

   _____.

5. preparar / Yo / la cena

   _____.

2-46 ▶ ¿Cúal es la pregunta? You are listening to your friend as she talks on the telephone. Reconstruct the questions of the person she is talking to, based on the answers she gives.

Modelo: *¿A qué hora tienes la clase de ciencias políticas?*
          Tengo la clase de ciencias políticas a las nueve de la mañana.

1. _____

   Ana y Marta son mis amigas de la universidad.

2. _____

   Voy a ir al cine con Ana y Marta.

3. _____

   Voy a la biblioteca porque tengo un examen mañana.

4. _____

   Mi residencia está al lado del centro estudiantil.

5. _____

   Tengo cuatro clases este semestre.

En la vida real
Context for activities 2-47 to 2-52

A group of prospective students is coming to visit your university and you will be their tour guide. You will have to answer questions not only about the university campus and the classes, but also about the city where the university is located and the possible activities students can do after class.

2-47 ▶ La visita. You are explaining to the visitors how the visit will be organized and what you will do. Put the following statements in chronological order.

1. Vamos a ver dónde están la biblioteca, el centro estudiantil y la cafetería. _____

2. En el centro de la ciudad, vamos a ver dónde hay muchos cafés, tiendas, restaurantes y clubes nocturnos. _____

3. Primero (*First*), vamos a hacer un tour del campus de la universidad. _____

4. Finalmente, vamos a tener tiempo para contestar sus preguntas. _____

5. Después de visitar la universidad, vamos a pasear por la ciudad. _____

6. Después de comer en la cafetería, vamos a ver los salones de clase de la Facultad de Ciencias. _____

2-48 ▶ Los días de clase. The students have a lot of questions related to the class schedules and the various possibilities the university offers. Answer the following questions in complete sentences.

1. ¿De qué hora a qué hora hay clases?

   _____

2. ¿Hay clases todos los días de la semana?

   _____

3. ¿Hay clases los fines de semana?

   _____

4. ¿Con qué frecuencia hay clases de español?

   _____

5. ¿Cómo son las clases? ¿Son difíciles?

   _____

2-49 ▶ El campus universitario y sus alredededores. During your tour, you are explaining where the following buildings of the university and its surroundings are located. Complete the sentences with the correct words or phrases from the list.

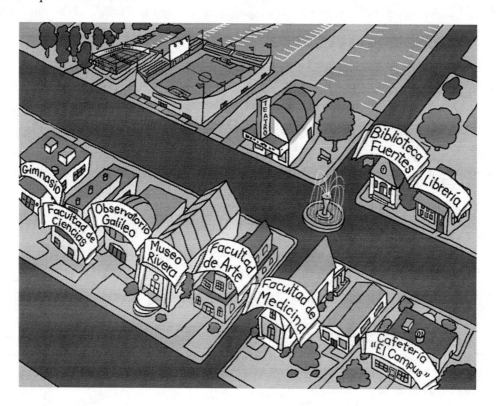

entre	a la izquierda de	enfrente de	lejos de	a la derecha del

1. El teatro está _____ estadio.

2. La biblioteca Fuentes está _____ la librería.

3. La Facultad de Medicina está _____ la biblioteca.

4. El museo Rivera está _____ el Observatorio Galileo y la Facultad de Arte.

5. El gimnasio está _____ la librería.

2-50 ▶ Preguntas. The following are a few questions that some of the new students ask. Fill in the missing question words based on the answers provided.

1. — ¿ _____ está el gimnasio?

   — Está al lado de la biblioteca.

2. — ¿ _____ clases tienen los estudiantes cada (*each*) semestre?

   — Generalmente los estudiantes tienen cuatro o cinco clases cada semestre.

3. — ¿ _____ estudias en esta universidad?

— Porque me gustan los profesores.

4. — ¿ _____ te gusta más de la universidad?

— Me gusta más el horario flexible de las clases.

5. — ¿ _____ es tu profesor favorito?

— Mi profesor favorito es el profesor de historia.

6. — ¿ _____ es tu clase favorita?

— Mi clase favorita es la clase de ciencias.

2-51 ▶ Ahora tú. Listen to the following six questions, and give your answers orally. Remember to use complete sentences.

1. . . .   3. . . .   5. . . .

2. . . .   4. . . .   6. . . .

2-52 ▶ Actividades fuera de clase. Your group of visitors also wants to know what kind of activities the students at your university do after class. Look at the drawings and complete the sentences with the verb phrases from the word bank. Remember to conjugate the verbs correctly.

tomar café	**estudiar en la biblioteca**	**nadar en la piscina**	**mirar la televisión**
escuchar música	**comprar libros**	*bailar en los clubes nocturnos*	

Modelo:

En la universidad, muchos estudiantes *bailan en los clubes nocturnos.*

1. Cada mañana, yo

_____.

2. En la universidad, muchos estudiantes

_____.

3. Mis amigos casi nunca

_____ .

5. Mi compañero de cuarto siempre

_____ .

4. Con frecuencia, mis amigos y yo

_____ .

6. A veces mis amigos y yo

_____ .

Lectores de hoy

2-53 ▶ **¿Qué significa?** Read the text about Spanish students and guess the meaning of the words below it using the context. Match each word with its English equivalent.

Los estudiantes españoles

En España, la vida (*life*) estudiantil es un poco diferente de la vida estudiantil en Estados Unidos. Los estudiantes no viven en el campus universitario como los estudiantes norteamericanos. Generalmente, viven en casa de sus padres o alquilan un cuarto en una residencia estudiantil o en un apartamento.

Van a clase en moto o en transporte público. Por lo general, no tienen coche (*car*). Durante la semana, van a clase todos los días. No tienen clases los fines de semana. Por la tarde, van a tomar café con sus amigos o estudian en la biblioteca. Otros van al gimnasio a hacer deporte. Normalmente, los deportes están separados de la universidad. No es como en Estados Unidos donde la universidad tiene sus propios (*their own*) equipos.

Por la noche, los estudiantes españoles salen de fiesta. Van a tomar algo en los bares cerca de la universidad. Después, salen a bailar. A veces no regresan a casa hasta muy tarde (*late*). Los fines de semana, algunos (*some*) van de compras, y otros van al cine o a un concierto. Siempre están muy ocupados.

1. viven _____
2. alquilan _____
3. padres _____
4. equipo _____
5. salen de fiesta _____

a. *parents*
b. *team*
c. (*they*) *rent*
d. (*they*) *go out partying*
e. (*they*) *live*

2-54 ▶ ¿Cierto o Falso? Based on the reading in **2-53**, indicate whether the following statements about students and universities in Spain are **cierto** or **falso.** Select **No se menciona** if it is not mentioned.

1. Los estudiantes españoles viven en el campus de la universidad.

   Cierto   Falso   No se menciona.

2. Todos los estudiantes españoles tienen una moto.

   Cierto   Falso   No se menciona.

3. Van en moto o en transporte público a la universidad.

   Cierto   Falso   No se menciona.

4. Van a clase tres veces a la semana.

   Cierto   Falso   No se menciona.

5. Tienen clase los sábados.

   Cierto   Falso   No se menciona.

6. Normalmente, las universidades españolas no tienen sus propios equipos de deporte.

   Cierto   Falso   No se menciona.

7. Los estudiantes españoles nunca salen de fiesta.

   Cierto   Falso   No se menciona.

8. Los estudiantes españoles están aburridos.

   Cierto   Falso   No se menciona.

2-55 ▶ ¿Tienes preguntas? Some Spanish students are coming to visit your university. You will have a chance to ask them a few questions about their student life. Write five questions that you would ask them.

1. _____

2. _____

3. _____

4. _____

5. _____

Voces de la calle

2-56 ▶ Unas preguntas generales. Watch the video as many times as necessary, and match each question with the best answer.

1. ¿Cuántas personas hablan en el video? _____

   a. Tiene veinticinco años.

2. ¿De dónde es Jane Delgado? _____

   b. Es una escuela y un centro de teatro.

3. ¿Qué es el Abrons Arts Center? _____

   c. Los 30 años del centro.

4. ¿Qué va a celebrar el Abrons Arts Center? _____

   d. Es de Nueva York.

5. ¿Cuántos años tiene (*How old is*) el Teatro Pregones? _____

   e. Dos personas hablan.

Nombre: _____   Fecha: _____

2-57 ▶ ¿Cierto o Falso? Read the following statements about the Abrons Arts Center and the Teatro Pregones and decide whether they are **Cierto** or **Falso.**

1. El Abrons Arts Center se dedica a las artes.   Cierto   Falso

2. Los alumnos tienen entre 2 y 87 años.   Cierto   Falso

3. Los alumnos son todos del vecindario (*neighborhood*).   Cierto   Falso

4. El teatro Pregones presenta solamente obras (*plays*)
   puertorriqueñas.   Cierto   Falso

5. El teatro Pregones presenta teatro contemporáneo.   Cierto   Falso

Escritores en acción

2-58 ▶ El periódico de la universidad. Your university newspaper has asked you to write an introductory article for prospective students in Spanish. Think about what you would have liked to have known before your first semester and what you think you should tell new students who will study at your university. Use the brainstorming strategy to think first about what you will say. Topics that you might want to include in your article are the location of the university, the students, the classes and class schedules, the professors, and activities to do on and off campus.

_____

_____

_____

_____

_____

_____

_____

_____

_____

Capítulo 2

VOCABULARIO

¿Cómo es tu horario?

- Assessment Goal: Vocabulary

- Topic: Mi horario

- Response Type: Essay

- Machine Gradable: No

Indicate where you usually are at the following days and times. Be sure to write out the time in words, as shown in the model.

MODELO: los lunes a las 8:30 de la mañana

Los lunes a las ocho y media de la mañana estoy en la cama.

1. los martes a la 1:00 de la tarde

_____

2. los miércoles a las 9:15 de la mañana

_____

3. los jueves a las 8:30 de la noche

_____

4. los viernes a las 4:45 de la tarde

_____

5. los sábados a las 10:00 de la noche

_____

6. los domingos a las 2:20 de la tarde

_____

Answers:

Answers will vary. Possible answers:

1. Los martes a la una de la tarde estoy en la cafetería.

2. Los miércoles a las nueve y cuarto de la mañana estoy en clase.

3. Los jueves a las ocho y media de la noche estoy en la biblioteca.

4. Los viernes a las cinco menos cuarto de la tarde estoy en el café con mis amigos.

5. Los sábados a las diez de la noche estoy en el club.

6. Los domingos a las dos y veinte de la tarde estoy en casa.

¿Quieres estudiar en la biblioteca?

- Assessment Goal: Vocabulary

- Topic: Las actividades diarias

- Response Type: Matching

- Machine Gradable: Yes

Match each item with the appropriate response to form a logical conversation.

_____1. ¿Quieres estudiar en la biblioteca hoy?   a. Trabajo de cuatro a diez de la

noche.

_____2. ¿Hasta qué hora estás en clase?   b. Muy bien, hasta el domingo.

_____3. Y después de la clase, ¿a las cuatro?   c. Estoy en clase desde las once

hasta las cuatro.

_____4. ¿Y el fin de semana?   d. El domingo está bien.

_____5. ¿A las tres y media el domingo, entonces? e. Hoy no puedo, tengo clase.

Answers:

1. e

2. c

3. a

4. d

5. b

Los fines de semana

- Assessment Goal: Vocabulary

- Topic: Las actividades diarias

- Response Type: Fill in the blanks

- Machine Gradable: Yes

Complete the following conversation with the logical expression from the list.

ir a bailar   comer   ir al cine   mirar un DVD

salir con mis amigos   pasar la noche   tomar algo

ARTURO: ¿Qué te gusta hacer los fines de semana?

AIDA: Los viernes casi siempre estoy cansada. Trabajo hasta las siete y después del

trabajo, no quiero salir y prefiero (1)_____ en casa.

ARTURO: ¿No trabajas los sábados ni los domingos?

AIDA: No, los sábados me gusta (2) _____. Paso mucho tiempo con

ellos. Me gusta (3) _____ a ver una película. A veces me gusta (4)

_____ en un restaurante.

ARTURO: ¿Te gusta descansar los domingos?

AIDA: Sí, me gusta (5) _____ en la televisión, pero casi siempre necesito hacer mucha tarea. ¿Y tú? ¿Qué haces los fines de semana?

ARTURO: Pues, me gusta pasar tiempo con mis amigos también. Generalmente, los sábados por la noche prefiero (6) _____ en un club nocturno, y los domingos por la tarde me gusta (7) _____ en un café.

Answers:

1. pasar la noche

2. salir con mis amigos

3. ir al cine

4. comer / tomar algo

5. mirar un DVD

6. ir a bailar

7. tomar algo / comer

Preferencias

- Assessment Goal: Vocabulary

- Topic: Lugares cerca de la universidad

- Response Type: Fill in the blanks

- Machine Gradable: Yes

Aida is describing what she likes to do on the weekends. Complete her description with the correct words from the list.

el estadio	un club nocturno	el cine	la librería
un restaurante	un parque		

Hola, me llamo Aida y soy de Caracas. Durante la semana tengo cuatro clases, y los viernes por la noche trabajo. A veces los sábados por la tarde hay partidos de fútbol americano en el campus, y me gusta ir. Prefiero ver el fútbol en (1)

_____ y no en la tele. Los sábados por la noche siempre hay fiestas en casa de mis amigos. Prefiero bailar en casa de mis amigos, pero a veces bailamos en (2)

_____ también. Los domingos por la mañana me gusta comer fuera (*out*); prefiero comer en (3) _____ y no cocinar en casa. Otras veces, voy de picnic con mis amigos a (4) _____. Los domingos por la tarde me gusta descansar y prefiero ver un DVD en casa, pero a veces prefiero ver una película en (5)

_____. A veces los domingos me gusta salir a comprar libros; prefiero comprar libros en (6) _____, y no por Internet.

Answers:

1. el estadio

2. un club nocturno

3. un restaurante

4. un parque

5. el cine

6. la librería

Tu fin de semana

- Assessment Goal: Vocabulary

- Topic: Los pasatiempos

- Response Type: Essay

- Machine Gradable: No

Answer each of the following questions in 3–4 complete sentences. Be sure to mention different activities for each question.

1. ¿Qué te gusta hacer después de clase? ¿Adónde vas para hacer esas (*those*) actividades?

_____

_____

2. ¿Qué te gusta hacer los fines de semana? ¿Adónde vas para hacer esas (*those*) actividades?

_____

_____

3. ¿Qué actividades prefieres hacer solo/a? ¿Qué actividades prefieres hacer con tus amigos?

_____

_____

Answers:

Answers will vary.

GRAMÁTICA

¿Qué hora es?

- Assessment Goal: Grammar

- Topic: *Describing your schedule: Time and the days of the week*

- Response Type: Fill in the blanks

- Machine Gradable: Yes

Say what time it is on each clock, and write the time out in words. Be sure to indicate also whether it is morning, afternoon, or evening, following the model exactly.

MODELO:

Son las once y media de la mañana.

1. _____.

2. _____.

3. _____.

4. _____.

5. _____.

6. _____.

7. _____.

8. _____.

Answers:

1. Es la una y diez de la tarde.

2. Son las diez menos cuarto de la noche. / Son las diez menos quince de la noche. / Son las nueve y cuarenta y cinco de la noche.

3. Son las nueve menos diez de la mañana. / Son las ocho y cincuenta de la mañana.

4. Son las once y veinticinco de la mañana.

5. Son las dos menos veinte de la tarde. / Es la una y cuarenta de la tarde.

6. Son las diez y cuarto de la noche. / Son las diez y quince de la noche.

7. Son las siete y veinticinco de la mañana.

8. Es la una menos cinco de la tarde. / Son las doce y cincuenta y cinco de la tarde.

Horarios

- Assessment Goal: Grammar

- Topic: *Describing your schedule: Time and the days of the week*

- Response Type: Fill in the blanks

- Machine Gradable: Yes

Convert the following show times from the 24-hour clock to conversational time, and write them out in words. Use **es** or **son** as appropriate, and indicate whether it is morning, afternoon, or evening.

MODELO: 17:00

Son las cinco de la tarde.

1. 16:00 _____.

2. 21:30 _____.

3. 12:45 _____.

4. 15:10 _____.

5. 22:35 _____.

6. 14:50 _____.

Answers:

1. Son las cuatro de la tarde.

2. Son las nueve y media de la noche. / Son las nueve y treinta de la noche.

3. Es la una menos cuarto de la tarde. / Son las doce y cuarenta y cinco de la tarde. / Es la una menos quince de la tarde.

4. Son las tres y diez de la tarde.

5. Son las once menos veinticinco de la noche. / Son las diez y treinta y cinco de la noche.

6. Son las tres menos diez de la tarde. / Son las dos y cincuenta de la tarde.

¿Tienes clase hoy?

- Assessment Goal: Grammar

- Topic: *Describing your schedule: Time and the days of the week*

- Response Type: Fill in the blanks

- Machine Gradable: Yes

Complete the following conversation with logical prepositions from the list. Prepositions may be used more than once.

a   de   hasta   por

ARTURO: Hola Aida, ¿tienes clase hoy (1) _____ la tarde?

AIDA: Sí, tengo clase de química (2) _____ tres (3) _____ cuatro y media. ¿Y tú?

ARTURO: No, los lunes no tengo clase (4) _____ la tarde. Mis clases son (5) _____ lunes (6) _____ viernes (7) _____ la mañana.

AIDA: ¿Te gustaría estudiar conmigo en la biblioteca?

ARTURO: Sí, está bien. ¿(8) _____ qué hora?

AIDA: ¿(9) _____ las siete?

ARTURO: Sí, (10) _____ luego, entonces.

Answers:

1. por

2. de

3. a

4. por

5. de

6. a

7. por

8. A

9. A

10. hasta

¿Te gustaría estudiar juntos?

- Assessment Goal: Grammar

- Topic: *Describing your schedule: Time and the days of the week*

- Response Type: Multiple choice

- Machine Gradable: Yes

Complete the following conversation between Marco and Juan by selecting the correct word in parentheses.

MARCO: ¿Trabajas más (1. de/por) la mañana este semestre?

JUAN: Sólo tengo historia (2. el/los) martes y jueves (3. son/a) las nueve de la mañana.

MARCO: Yo tengo más clases (4. de/por) la tarde. Mis clases de filosofía, inglés y arte son (5. el/los) lunes, miércoles y viernes (6. a/de) dos (7. a/de) cinco.

JUAN: Oye (*Hey*), unos amigos y yo vamos al lago (8. el/los) sábado. ¿Te gustaría ir con nosotros?

MARCO: 9.¿(De/A) qué hora?

JUAN: (10. A/Son) las dos (11. de/por) la tarde.

MARCO: Está bien. ¡Sí, me gustaría!

Answers:

1. por

2. los

3. a

4. por

5. los

6. de

7. a

8. el

9. A

10. A

11. de

Tu horario

- Assessment Goal: Grammar

- Topic: *Describing your schedule: Time and the days of the week*

- Response Type: Essay

- Machine Gradable: No

Answer each of the following questions in 3–4 complete sentences.

1. ¿Te gusta tu horario este semestre/trimestre? ¿Qué días son tus clases?

_____

_____

2. ¿A qué hora prefieres tener tus clases? ¿A qué hora es tu clase de español?

_____

_____

3. ¿Qué día(s) trabajas? ¿Te gusta tu horario de trabajo?

_____

_____

Answers:

Answers will vary.

¿Dónde estás generalmente?

- Assessment Goal: Grammar

- Topic: *Saying where you are: The verb **estar***

- Response Type: Fill in the blanks

- Machine Gradable: Yes

Complete Aida and Arturo's conversation with the correct forms of the verb **estar**.

AIDA: Arturo, ¿dónde (1) _____ (tú) generalmente antes de la clase de español?

ARTURO: (2) _____ en la biblioteca. ¿Y tú?

AIDA: Mi compañera Lidia y yo (3) _____ en la clase de química.

ARTURO: Y después de la clase, ¿dónde (4) _____ ustedes?

AIDA: Generalmente, en casa.

ARTURO: ¿(5) _____ la casa cerca del campus?

AIDA: Sí. Me gusta (6) _____ cerca de las clases y la biblioteca.

Answers:

1. estás

2. Estoy

3. estamos

4. están

5. Está

6. estar

Rutinas

- Assessment Goal: Grammar

- Topic: *Saying where you are: The verb **estar***

- Response Type: Fill in the blanks

- Machine Gradable: Yes

Complete the following sentences with the correct form of **estar** in the first blank and a logical place in the second one.

el club nocturno	el gimnasio	la iglesia	la sinagoga
la mezquita	la biblioteca	el estadio	la oficina

1. Yo siempre _____ en _____ con mis amigos los sábados por la noche. Me gusta bailar.

2. Generalmente mis amigos y yo _____ en _____ los sábados por la tarde para ver un partido de fútbol americano.

3. Mi compañero de cuarto siempre _____ en _____ los domingos por la mañana. Es muy religioso.

4. Generalmente mis compañeros de clase _____ en _____ antes de clase. Estudian juntos.

5. ¿Trabajas los fines de semana? ¿Hasta qué hora _____ en

_____ los sábados?

6. ¿Tus amigos y tú levantan pesas todos los días? ¿A qué hora _____ en

_____?

Answers:

1. estoy, el club nocturno

2. estamos, el estadio

3. está, la iglesia/la mezquita/la sinagoga

4. están, la biblioteca

5. estás, la oficina

6. están/ estáis, el gimnasio

Tu rutina de la semana

- Assessment Goal: Grammar

- Topic: *Saying where you are: The verb **estar***

- Response Type: Essay

- Machine Gradable: No

Answer each of the following questions in 1–2 complete sentences.

1. ¿De qué hora a qué hora estás en clase todos los días? ¿Qué días no estás en la

universidad?

_____

_____

2. Generalmente, ¿cuándo estás en la biblioteca? ¿Prefieres estar en la biblioteca o en casa después de las clases?

_____

_____

3. ¿Estás generalmente con tus amigos por la noche, o prefieres estar solo/a?

_____

_____

Answers:

Answers will vary.

Acciones

- Assessment Goal: Grammar

- Topic: *Talking about your activities: Regular -ar verbs*

- Response Type: Fill in the blanks

- Machine Gradable: Yes

Arturo is talking about what he and his friends do during the week and on the weekends. Complete his description with the appropriate form of each verb in parentheses.

Hola, soy Arturo y soy estudiante. Mis compañeros de cuarto y yo (1) _____ (estudiar) mucho durante la semana, y los fines de semana nosotros (2) _____ (pasar) tiempo juntos. Yo (3) _____ (trabajar) también los miércoles y los jueves en la oficina de mi padre, cuando él (4) _____ (necesitar) ayuda (*help*). Mis compañeros de cuarto no (5) _____ (trabajar), pero los jueves ellos generalmente (6) _____ (limpiar) el apartamento y (7) _____ (cocinar). Los sábados yo (8) _____ (descansar) por la mañana, y por la noche

me gusta salir a bailar con ellos a un club nocturno.

Answers:

1. estudiamos

2. pasamos

3. trabajo

4. necesita

5. trabajan

6. limpian

7. cocinan

8. descanso

A veces, nunca…

- Assessment Goal: Grammar

- Topic: *Talking about your activities: Regular **-ar** verbs*

- Response Type: Essay

- Machine Gradable: No

Answer the following questions about yourself in complete sentences.

1. ¿Llegas a la universidad antes de las siete de la mañana? ¿A qué hora llegas?

_____.

2. Generalmente, ¿qué días pasas en la universidad?

_____.

3. ¿Escuchas a los profesores con atención?

_____.

4. Generalmente, ¿llegan los profesores a clase a la hora? ¿Cuándo llegan?

_____.

5. A veces, ¿trabajan tus compañeros y tú juntos en proyectos de clase?

_____.

6. ¿Estudian tus compañeros y tú en la biblioteca con frecuencia?

_____.

Answers:

Answers will vary.

¿Hasta qué hora?

- Assessment Goal: Grammar

- Topic: *Talking about your activities: Regular* *-ar* *verbs*

- Response Type: Fill in the blanks

- Machine Gradable: Yes

Complete the following conversation with the correct form of the appropriate verbs from the list.

| estar | mirar | comprar | preparar | regresar |

| necesitar | estudiar | pasar |

MARCOS: Ramón, ¿a qué hora (1) _____ a casa del trabajo, generalmente?

RAMÓN: A las seis y media. (2) _____ todo el día en la oficina y luego (3) _____ comida en el supermercado antes de llegar a casa.

MARCOS: ¿(4) _____ la cena todos los días, o te gusta comer fuera (*out*) a veces?

RAMÓN: Me gusta comer en un restaurante a veces si (*if*) (5) _____ cansado

y (6) _____ descansar.

MARCOS: ¿Te gusta mirar la televisión por la noche?

RAMÓN: Sí, con frecuencia (7) _____ la tele un poco antes de dormir (*to sleep*).

MARCOS: ¿Y cuándo (8) _____?

RAMÓN: Generalmente, estudio los fines de semana. ¡Estoy bien ocupado!

Answers:

1. regresas

2. Paso

3. compro

4. Preparas

5. estoy

6. necesito

7. miro

8. estudias

Actividades

- Assessment Goal: Grammar

- Topic: *Talking about your activities: Regular **-ar** verbs*

- Response Type: Essay

- Machine Gradable: No

Say how often each of these people does the activity pictured. Use an **–ar** verb in each statement with one of the adverbs of frequency from the list to write descriptive sentences.

todos los días   con frecuencia   a veces   (casi) nunca

hablar por teléfono

MODELO:

Mi mamá habla por teléfono todos los días.

**mirar partidos de básquetbol
en la televisión**

1. Mi mejor amigo/a _____.

limpiar la casa

2. Mis amigos _____.

preparar la cena

3. Mi papá _____.

escuchar música y bailar

4. Mis amigos también_____.

estudiar

5. Yo _____.

Answers:

Answers will vary.

Preguntas personales

- Assessment Goal: Grammar

- Topic: *Talking about your activities: Regular **-ar** verbs*

- Response Type: Essay

- Machine Gradable: No

Answer each of the following questions in 1-2 complete sentences.

1. Generalmente, ¿a qué hora llegas a la universidad? ¿A qué hora regresas a casa?

_____

2. ¿Estudias con frecuencia en la biblioteca, o prefieres estudiar en casa? ¿Por qué?

_____

3. ¿Estudias con tus compañeros, o prefieres estudiar solo/a?

_____

4. ¿Te gusta comer en la cafetería, o prefieres preparar comida en casa?

_____

5. ¿Miras un poco la tele por la noche? ¿Con qué frecuencia?

_____

6. ¿Bailas en un club nocturno, o prefieres descansar en tu tiempo libre?

_____

Answers:

Answers will vary.

¿Qué o cuál(es)?

- Assessment Goal: Grammar

- Topic: *Asking questions: Question formation*

- Response Type: Fill in the blanks

- Machine Gradable: Yes

Complete the following questions for your instructor with **qué** or **cuál(es)**.

1. ¿ _____ es la tarea para el lunes?

2. ¿ _____ necesitamos estudiar para mañana?

3. ¿ _____ es una expresión interrogativa?

4. ¿ _____ son las palabras que debemos estudiar para el examen?

5. ¿ _____ más necesitamos estudiar para el examen?

6. ¿ _____ significa el verbo **regresar**?

Answers:

1. Cuál

2. Qué

3. Qué

4. Cuáles

5. Qué

6. Qué

¿Cuál es la pregunta?

- Assessment Goal: Grammar

- Topic: *Asking questions: Question formation*

- Response Type: Essay

- Machine Gradable: No

Write the question that was most likely asked in order to get the following answers.

1. _____

La profesora de español es la señora Blanco.

2. _____

La señora Blanco es de Caracas.

3. _____

La clase de la señora Blanco es muy interesante.

4. _____

La señora Blanco está en su (*her*) oficina los lunes y los miércoles después de clase.

5. _____

Estudio con mi mejor amigo para la clase de español.

6. _____

Mi mejor amigo y yo trabajamos juntos en la biblioteca.

Answers:

Answers may vary. Possible answers:

1. ¿Quién es la profesora de español?

2. ¿De dónde es la señora Blanco?

3. ¿Cómo es la clase de la señora Blanco?

4. ¿Cuándo está la señora Blanco en su oficina?

5. ¿Con quién estudias para la clase de español?

6. ¿Dónde trabajan tu mejor amigo y tú?

Preguntas

- Assessment Goal: Grammar

- Topic: *Asking questions: Question formation*

- Response Type: Essay

- Machine Gradable: No

Write six questions that you would like to ask your Spanish teacher using different interrogative words in each.

MODELO: *¿Qué días trabaja usted?*

1. _____

2. _____

3. _____

4. _____

5. _____

6. _____

Answers:

Answers will vary.

Mi residencia

- Assessment Goal: Grammar

- Topic: *Indicating location: Prepositions of place and contractions with **de***

- Response Type: Fill in the blanks

- Machine Gradable: Yes

Complete the following sentences with the correct prepositions. Be sure to insert the article when needed.

1. Este semestre vivo (*live*) _____ (*in*) una residencia muy bonita

_____ (*on*) el campus.

2. La residencia está _____ (*behind the*) biblioteca y _____ (*next to the*) gimnasio.

3. La habitación de mi mejor amigo está _____ (*to the right of*) mi

habitación, y yo paso mucho tiempo _____ (*with*) él.

4. El edificio de clases está _____ (*near*) la residencia, y puedo (*I can*) ir

_____ (*without*) mi coche.

5. La universidad no está _____ (*far from the*) centro de la ciudad, y el

autobús pasa _____ (*in front of the*) la residencia.

Answers:

1. en, en

2. detrás de la, al lado del

3. a la derecha de, con

4. cerca de, sin

5. lejos del, delante de

¿Dónde está tu oficina?

- Assessment Goal: Grammar

- Topic: *Indicating location: Prepositions of place and contractions with* **de**

- Response Type: Fill in the blanks

- Machine Gradable: Yes

Complete the following conversation with the logical prepositions from the list. The prepositions may be used more than once.

lejos de   con   entre   en   cerca de

JULIO: ¿Trabajas (1) _____ aquí?

LIDIA: Sí, llego al trabajo en diez minutos.

JULIO: ¿Está la oficina (2) _____ el centro de la ciudad?

LIDIA: Sí, está (3) _____ la calle Argüelles y la avenida Marqués de Urquijo.

JULIO: ¿(4) _____ qué edificio está tu oficina?

LIDIA: En el edificio Miravalles. Está (5) _____ la librería Urquijo.

JULIO: Y ¿estás contenta (6) _____ tu trabajo?

LIDIA: Sí, es interesante y trabajo bien (7) _____ mis compañeros.

JULIO: ¡Qué bueno! Mi trabajo no es interesante y está muy (8) _____ aquí, al otro lado de la ciudad.

Answers:

1. cerca de

2. en

3. entre

4. En

5. cerca de

6. en/con

7. con

8. lejos de

¿Dónde está…?

- Assessment Goal: Grammar

- Topic: *Indicating location: Prepositions of place and contractions with **de***

- Response Type: Essay

- Machine Gradable: No

Answer each of the following questions in at least two complete sentences.

1. ¿Dónde está tu apartamento/residencia? ¿Está cerca de la universidad?

_____

_____

2. ¿Dónde está tu salón de clase? ¿Tomas todas las clases en el mismo (*same*) salón?

_____

_____

3. ¿Está tu universidad lejos del centro de la ciudad? ¿Entre qué calle(s) está tu

universidad?

_____

_____

Answers:

Answers will vary.

¿Adónde vas para…?

- Assessment Goal: Grammar

- Topic: *Saying what you are going to do: **Ir**, contractions with **a**, **ir a** + infinitive*

- Response Type: Matching

- Machine Gradable: Yes

Form logical sentences by combining the elements from the two columns. Be sure to watch for correct subject-verb agreement using **ir.**

1. Para mirar una película, yo ____	a. vamos a un club nocturno.
2. Para estudiar, mis compañeros y yo____	b. voy a una librería.
3. Para bailar, mis amigos y yo____	c. voy al cine.
4. Para hablar con la profesora, tú____	d. van a la piscina.
5. Para nadar, mis padres____	e. vas a su (*her*) oficina.
6. Para comprar libros, yo ____	f. vamos a la biblioteca.

Answers:

1. c

2. f

3. a

4. e

5. d

6. b

¿Con qué frecuencia?

- Assessment Goal: Grammar

- Topic: *Saying what you are going to do:* **Ir,** *contractions with* **a, ir a** + *infinitive*

- Response Type: Essay

- Machine Gradable: No

Form sentences using the verb **ir** with the words provided and an adverb of frequency from the list.

(casi) siempre   todos los días   con frecuencia   a veces   (casi) nunca

MODELO: los sábados por la tarde, yo / el estadio

Los sábados por la tarde, yo voy a veces al estadio.

1. después de clase, mis amigos y yo / el gimnasio

_____

2. antes de clase, mi profesor/a de español / su oficina

_____

3. yo / un restaurante de comida argentina

_____

4. los jueves por la noche, mis compañeros / un club nocturno

_____

5. los domingos por la tarde, mis amigos y yo / el cine

_____

6. los fines de semana, el profesor Santos / la biblioteca

_____

Answers:

Answers will vary. Possible answers:

1. Después de clase, mis amigos y yo vamos a veces al gimnasio.

2. Antes de clase, mi profesor de español va siempre a su oficina.

3. Yo casi nunca voy a un restaurante de comida argentina.

4. Los jueves por la noche, mis compañeros van casi siempre a un club nocturno.

5. Los domingos por la tarde, mis amigos y yo vamos con frecuencia al cine.

6. Los fines de semana, el profesor Santos va a veces a la biblioteca.

¿Adónde vas?

- Assessment Goal: Grammar

- Topic: *Saying what you are going to do:* **Ir,** *contractions with* **a,** **ir a** *+ infinitive*

- Response Type: Essay

- Machine Gradable: No

Answer the following questions about yourself.

1. ¿Adónde vas generalmente los fines de semana?

_____

2. ¿Con qué frecuencia van tus amigos y tú al cine?

_____

3. ¿Con qué frecuencia vas al centro comercial?

_____

4. ¿Adónde van tus compañeros y tú para estudiar?

_____

5. ¿Vas a la oficina de tu profesor/a de español a veces?

_____

6. ¿Adónde vas generalmente después de las clases?

_____

Answers:

Answers will vary.

¿Qué van a hacer?

- Assessment Goal: Grammar

- Topic: *Saying what you are going to do: **Ir**, contractions with **a**, **ir a** + infinitive*

- Response Type: Essay

- Machine Gradable: No

Say that the indicated people are going to the place shown. Then use the immediate future to write a logical sentence saying what they are going to do there.

MODELO: Mi amigo *va al centro comercial. Va a comprar algo.*

**un cine con películas
extranjeras
(de aventuras, de terror)**

1. Mis amigos y yo

_____.

2. Muchos estudiantes

_____.

3. Mi compañero de de cuarto

_____.

un supermercado

4. Yo _____.

un restaurante (de comida mexicana,
de comida italiana)

5. Mi mamá y mi papá _____.

Answers:

Answers will vary. Possible answers:

1. vamos al cine. Vamos a ver una película.

2. van al estadio. Van a ver un partido de fútbol.

3. va al lago, Va a nadar y hacer esquí acuático.

4. voy al supermercado. Voy a comprar comida.

5. van a un restaurante. Van a comer.

¡A ESCUCHAR!

[Audio icon] **¿Qué días estás en clase?**

- Assessment Goal: Listening

- Topic: *Identifying the main idea*

- Response Type: Essay

- Machine Gradable: No

Listen to the following conversation, and answer the questions in complete sentences.

1. ¿Qué días está Lidia en la clase de español?

_____

2. ¿Qué días está Lidia en la clase de biología?

_____

3. ¿Cuántas horas trabaja Lidia el martes y jueves?

_____

4. ¿Trabaja Lidia también otros días esta semana?

_____

5. ¿Qué día van a estudiar juntos Julio y Lidia?

_____

6. ¿A qué hora van a estudiar los amigos?

_____

Answers:

Answers may vary. Possible answers:

1. Lidia está en clase la de español los lunes, miércoles y viernes.

2. Lidia está en la clase de biología los martes y jueves.

3. Lidia trabaja cinco horas el martes y jueves.

4. Sí, Lidia trabaja también todo el día el domingo.

5. Julio y Lidia van a estudiar juntos el viernes.

6. Los amigos van a estudiar a la una.

Audioscript

JULIO: Hola, Lidia. ¿Te gusta tu horario este semestre? ¿Qué días tienes clases?

LIDIA: Tengo clases de español, arte y filosofía los lunes, miércoles y viernes, y mi clase

de biología es los martes y jueves.

JULIO: ¿A qué hora son tus clases?

LIDIA: Los martes y jueves, mi clase de biología es a las once. Los lunes, miércoles y

viernes estoy en clase de nueve a doce.

JULIO: ¡Estás muy ocupada! ¿Trabajas también?

LIDIA: Sí, esta semana trabajo cinco horas el martes y jueves y todo el día el domingo.

Con frecuencia trabajo los viernes también, pero esta semana no trabajo el viernes.

JULIO: ¿Te gustaría estudiar conmigo el viernes?

LIDIA: Sí, me gustaría estudiar juntos. No me gusta estudiar sola. ¿A qué hora?

JULIO: No demasiado temprano… ¿a la una?

LIDIA: Está bien.

[Audio icon] **No es cierto.**

- Assessment Goal: Listening

- Topic: *Identifying the main idea*

- Response Type: Multiple choice

- Machine Gradable: Yes

Listen to Lidia as she talks about her schedule, and complete the sentences with the correct information.

1. Lidia está en la clase de filosofía…

a. los martes y los jueves.

b. los lunes, miércoles y viernes.

c. los lunes y los jueves.

2. Lidia está en clase…

a. los lunes, martes y viernes de nueve a doce.

b. los lunes, miércoles y viernes de diez a una.

c. los lunes, miércoles y viernes de nueve a doce.

3. La clase de biología es…

a. los martes y los jueves a las once.

b. los miércoles y los viernes a las once.

c. los lunes a las diez.

4. Lidia trabaja cinco horas…

a. los sábados.

b. los martes y los jueves.

c. los martes y los viernes.

5. Lidia nunca trabaja todo el día…

a. los domingos.

b. los martes y los viernes

c. los jueves y sábados.

6. Lidia y Julio van a estudiar…

a. el jueves a las doce.

b. el viernes a las seis.

c. el viernes a la una.

Answers

1. b

2. c

3. a

4. b

5. a

6. c

Audioscript

JULIO: Hola, Lidia. ¿Te gusta tu horario este semestre? ¿Qué días tienes clases?

LIDIA: Tengo clases de español, arte y filosofía los lunes, miércoles y viernes, y mi clase

de biología es los martes y jueves.

JULIO: ¿A qué hora son tus clases?

LIDIA: Los martes y jueves, mi clase de biología es a las once. Los lunes, miércoles y

viernes estoy en clase de nueve a doce.

JULIO: ¡Estás muy ocupada! ¿Trabajas también?

LIDIA: Sí, esta semana trabajo cinco horas el martes y jueves y todo el día el domingo.

Con frecuencia trabajo los viernes también, pero esta semana no trabajo el viernes.

JULIO: ¿Te gustaría estudiar conmigo el viernes?

LIDIA: Sí, me gustaría estudiar juntos. No me gusta estudiar sola. ¿A qué hora?

JULIO: No demasiado temprano… ¿a la una?

LIDIA: Está bien.

¿Qué falta?

- Assessment Goal: Listening

- Topic: *Identifying the main idea*

- Response Type: Fill in the blanks

- Machine Gradable: Yes

Listen to the following conversation, and fill in the missing words in the blanks.

JULIO: Bueno, Lidia. ¿Qué (1) _____ a hacer esta noche?

LIDIA: No sé. ¿Por qué no vamos al (2) _____?

JULIO: No, (3) _____ ir de compras. Necesito comprar un (4)

_____ para mi madre.

LIDIA: Está bien. ¿Vamos a (5) _____ después?

JULIO: Sí, ¿quieres ir al nuevo (6) _____ mexicano en la calle Mayor?

LIDIA: ¡Buena idea! ¿A qué hora (7) _____ por tu casa?

JULIO: ¿A las (8) _____?

LIDIA: No, mejor a las cinco.

JULIO: Está bien, hasta luego.

Answers:

1. vamos

2. cine

3. prefiero

4. regalo

5. comer

6. restaurante

7. paso

8. cuatro y media

Audioscript

JULIO: Bueno, Lidia. ¿Qué vamos a hacer esta noche?

LIDIA: No sé. ¿Por qué no vamos al cine?

JULIO: No, prefiero ir de compras. Necesito comprar un regalo para mi madre.

LIDIA: Está bien. ¿Vamos a comer después?

JULIO: Sí, ¿quieres ir al nuevo restaurante mexicano en la calle Mayor?

LIDIA: ¡Buena idea! ¿A qué hora paso por tu casa?

JULIO: ¿A las cuatro y media?

LIDIA: No, mejor a las cinco.

JULIO: Está bien, hasta luego.

Planes para esta noche

- Assessment Goal: Listening

- Topic: *Identifying the main idea*

- Response Type: Essay

- Machine Gradable: No

Listen to the following conversation, and answer the questions in complete sentences.

1. ¿Van Julio y Lidia al cine? ¿Adónde van?

_____

2. ¿Qué necesita Julio?

_____

3. ¿Adónde van los amigos después? ¿Dónde está?

_____

4. ¿A qué hora pasa Lidia por la casa de Julio?

_____

Answers:

Answers may vary. Possible answers:

1. No, Julio y Lidia no van al cine. Ellos van de compras.

2. Julio necesita comprar un regalo para su madre.

3. Los amigos van al nuevo restaurante mexicano. Está en la calle Mayor.

4. Lidia pasa por la casa de Julio a las cuatro y media.

Audioscript

JULIO: Bueno, Lidia. ¿Qué vamos a hacer esta noche?

LIDIA: No sé. ¿Por qué no vamos al cine?

JULIO: No, prefiero ir de compras. Necesito comprar un regalo para mi madre.

LIDIA: Está bien. ¿Vamos a comer después?

JULIO: Sí, ¿quieres ir al nuevo restaurante mexicano en la calle Mayor?

LIDIA: ¡Buena idea! ¿A qué hora paso por tu casa?

JULIO: ¿A las cuatro y media?

LIDIA: Muy bien. Hasta luego.

LECTORES DE HOY

¡Los mexicanos trabajan mucho!

- Assessment Goal: Reading

- Reading Strategy: *Guessing meaning from context*

- Response Type: Multiple choice

- Machine Gradable: Yes

Read the following report on the daily lives of people in Mexico, and use the context to determine the meaning of the following words found in the reading. Select the word that is a synonym for each word given.

Cada día, un mexicano promedio dedica 9,6 horas a estudiar o trabajar, revela una investigación de la Organización para la Cooperación y el Desarrollo Económicos que incluyó a 18 países, como Alemania, Estados Unidos, Francia y Turquía.

De los 18 países analizados, México es el que menos tiempo dedica al ocio, pues cada habitante invierte sólo 3,7 horas de su día en pasatiempos, juegos, deportes o sociabilización. Los mexicanos dedican casi el 50% de su tiempo libre a la televisión, pero son los que menos tiempo dedican a la comida. Apenas invierten una hora en comer, mientras que los franceses pasan más de dos horas en la mesa.

[Source: http://www.illac.com.mx/profiles/blogs/en-mexico-trabajan-mucho-y]

1. *promedio*   a. típico   b. religioso   c. aburrido

2. *países*	a. ciudades	b. compañías	c. naciones
3. *ocio*	a. diversiones	b. ejercicio	c. trabajo
4. *habitante*	a. residente	b. estudiante	c. casa
5. *invierte*	a. necesita	b. descansa	c. dedica
6. *apenas*	a. casi no	b. mucho más de	c. demasiado
7. *mientras*	a. porque	b. hasta	c. pero al mismo tiempo

Answers:

1. a

2. c

3. a

4. a

5. c

6. a

7. c

Costarricenses optan por pasatiempos baratos por la crisis.

- Assessment Goal: Reading

- Reading Strategy: *Guessing meaning from context*

- Response Type: Multiple choice

- Machine Gradable: Yes

Read the following report on leisure activities in Costa Rica, and use the context to determine the meaning of the words found in the reading. Select the word or phrase from those listed that could be substituted for each one.

Este año los costarricenses optan por actividades recreativas pasivas y baratas para su tiempo libre, como acudir a servicios religiosos y ver televisión en casa, reveló un sondeo de 701 personas realizado por teléfono en todo el país.

Participar en actividades religiosas (61%), ver televisión (60,8%), leer periódicos (56,8%), escuchar música en casa (52,4%), visitar a familiares o amigos (51,1%) y ver los partidos en la tele (46,2%) son las actividades recreativas más frecuentes en Costa Rica, según la encuesta de la Escuela de Estadística de la Universidad de Costa Rica. Un 53,5% de los costarricenses disminuye sus actividades recreativas debido a la situación económica. Sólo una minoría mantiene actividades más costosas, como tomar clases de baile (2,3%), ir al teatro (2,3%), ir a clases de deportes (2,6%), ir al prestigioso Teatro Nacional (2,7%) e ir a discotecas (2,8%).

[Source: http://www.diariolasamericas.com/pda_news.php?nid=63603]

1. *baratas*   a. divertidas   b. costosas   c. poco costosas

2. *acudir*   a. trabajar   b. ir   c. comer

3. *un sondeo*   a. un estudio   b. un concierto   c. un libro

4. *el país*   a. la nación   b. la calle   c. la oficina

5. *según*   a. afirma   b. pregunta   c. busca

6. *la encuesta* a. la opinión   b. la investigación   c. el criterio

7. *disminuye*   a. descansa   b. participa   c. reduce

8. *debido a*   a. cerca de   b. antes de   c. como resultado de

Answers:

1. c

2. b

3. a

4. a

5. a

6. b

7. c

8. c

ESCRITORES EN ACCIÓN

Mi horario

- Assessment Goal: Writing

- Topic: Mi horario

- Response Type: Essay

- Machine Gradable: No

Describe your weekly schedule. Talk about the classes that you have this semester, and the days and times when you are in class. If you work, be sure to provide information about your work schedule also. Use the following structures:

- **estar**

- **–ar** verbs

- expressions for saying the time and the days of the week

_____

_____

_____

_____

_____

_____

Answers

Answers will vary.

Después de clase

- Assessment Goal: Writing

- Topic: Las actividades diarias

- Response Type: Essay

- Machine Gradable: No

Describe the activities that you like to do after class. Talk about how often you do these activities and with whom. Use the following structures:

- –**ar** verbs

- vocabulary describing leisure activities and pastimes

_____

_____

_____

_____

_____

_____

Answers

Answers will vary.

Los fines de semana

- Assessment Goal: Writing

- Topic: Mi horario

- Response Type: Essay

- Machine Gradable: No

Describe the activities that you like to do on the weekends. Talk about how often you do these activities and with whom. Use the following structures:

- **ir**

- **–ar** verbs

- vocabulary describing leisure activities and pastimes

_____

_____

_____

_____

_____

Answers

Answers will vary.

Hablando de tu horario

- Assessment Goal: Speaking

- Topic: Mi horario

- Response Type: Essay – Voice recording

- Machine Gradable: No

Give an oral description of your class schedule this semester. Also mention the things you generally do after classes, and when you like to study at home or at the library.

Finally, tell whether you work, and if so, on what days.

Answers:

Answers will vary.

Los fines de semana

- Assessment Goal: Speaking

- Topic: Los pasatiempos

- Response Type: Essay – Voice recording

- Machine Gradable: No

Give an oral description of your typical weekend activities. Say whether you work, and if so, when. Then mention at least two places you go with your friends, how often, and what you do there. Finally, tell when you generally study for your classes.

Answers:

Answers will vary.